Having read over 100 books on these subjects it was a delight to find one that is practical, insightful, and anticipates the questions the reader will have. You will return to this excellent resource again and again to find your questions answered. The author has definitely done her homework. Whether you have just begun counseling, have been counseling for years, or are reading this as someone who has walked this journey, Surviving Trauma, Crisis & Grief will be at the top of your list.
- Dr H. Norman Wright, Traumatologist; author of *The Complete Guide to Crisis & Trauma Counseling*; former director of the Graduate Department of Marriage, Family and Child Counseling at Biola University

This book on trauma and crisis should have been written 25 years ago, when trauma was an almost non-existing topic in Christian circles. It was prayed away, or not acknowledged, or even worse, spiritualised as something you have to endure when you want to serve God. Thankfully this book is giving a wide understanding on what trauma is and the impact it can have on a person. You will find life-truth in this book, showing you that trauma is not your fault, and how you can help yourself get back to yourself and life.
- Martina Michaela Hoffmann, MSc, Psychological Counsellor

I love this book! It is well planned, written and laid out with Michelle's personal story supporting the validity of the content. If I had seen this when I was in the early stages of my trauma laden years, I would have devoured it in one. Understanding your journey of trauma and grief can be so debilitating, especially when the 'professionals' around you just can't grasp the depth of what you are living with and would rather send you off with the medication and tell you to get on with it! The content is broken down in such a way that it is easy to follow and there are many useful points that help to support the narrative. There are plenty of cross-references as you read your way through, and this supports you as you progress through the six informative chapters. I love the encouragement Michelle expresses in her writing. It is refreshing to find this kind of support in the written form.
- Debi Richens, Certified Grief Recovery Specialist

A very accessible book and super easy to read.
- Jenny Burns, Programme Lead Wales,
Mental Health Foundation

Dr. Simpson's excellent and practical steps to healing will be useful to trauma professionals as well as friends and acquaintances of victims. This book is not just a clinical guide, it is an excellent read for anyone who has personally suffered the effects of deep trauma or anyone who just wants to understand it better. Throughout the book, she is very encouraging and uplifting. I recommend this work wholeheartedly.
- Dr. Karen Drake, president,
Primus University of Theology International

Those who have experienced trauma need information and help that is simple, easy to read and understand, non-judgmental and filled with hope. Michelle has artfully and sensitively found the perfect balance. Reading this book creates a safe place for the traumatised, while giving a roadmap to the days ahead. Surviving Trauma is a "must-have" guide for everyone. For those who have suffered trauma and are dealing with its effects, it will help you navigate the unpredictable aftermath with more confidence and encouragement. For everyone else, it is an invaluable tool to understanding how to walk alongside those who are suffering and need the right support along the way. Trauma will continue to affect people and it's time to be informed so we can survive and thrive in its midst and make the world a kinder and more supportive space for those that need to heal.
As a health professional and someone that has experienced trauma myself, I appreciate and value the practical steps in this book.

- Rebecca Ramirez de Arellano, LMT
Founder and owner of Enci Wellness LLC

In her latest book, entitled, 'Surviving Trauma, Crisis & Grief', Dr Michelle Simpson shares her own personal experiences of the suffering and pain, caused by these debilitating conditions. Using her extensive clinical knowledge, undergirded by her strong Christian faith, Michelle offers very practical advice, tips and helps to enable the reader to begin on the road to recovery and ultimately to believing that there is a real hope and expectation of healing.
- Sue Allen, co-director, Caleb 14:24 Ministries

In a time where mental illness and health are trending, this is such an important relevant, informative and timely book! There is so much suffering from the affects of trauma, crisis and grief and many not sure or don't have all that is needed to SURVIVE! OVERCOME! In this book Michelle has offered some very good practical solutions that will help. Because of her own experience she's able to step right into your experience and touch those areas of pain with truth, acknowledgement, care, sensitivity and encouragement! Reading this book gave me validation and helped me acknowledge and put a name to what I was experiencing, which then led to more healing!

It's a good balance of practical and spiritual help. It's honest and sound. I was thinking of a few people I want to buy this book for. Well done Michelle for all the hard work in writing this book and sharing your heart with us. What the enemy meant for bad God is turning it around and using it for good!

Marsha Farmer, founder, Living Free

Michelle is an amazing woman who is surviving multiple traumas and with her unique giftedness in writing with courage and honesty has written this insightful book, full of wisdom gained in her own journey, to encourage those who are or have experienced trauma, and their relatives and close friends. For those experiencing trauma Michelle's insights, drawn from her own life experience, will permission you to recognise what has or is happening and give you hope and encouragement. For those seeking to walk with those in trauma, it will give you knowledge, understanding and practical help, that dealing with trauma is often more about choosing to survive than finding healing.

- Linda Harding, mentor, Simply Mobilizing; former European Director of World Outreach

An accessible and highly practical guide to working through trauma from both practical and spiritual perspectives. Michelle addresses the reader personally from the depths of her own struggles and thus offers no pat answers but ones discovered through her own experience and research on her journey dealing with C-PTSD. The book does not minimise the difficulties and pain of trauma and offers affirmation and encouragement to sufferers and those wishing to support them. As an experienced Christian Counsellor I welcome this book as an easy-to-read, useful and validating addition to the literature on surviving trauma.
- Kay Wells, BA (Hons), DipCo, PGDip Christian Mentoring

Surviving

Trauma, Crisis & Grief

Surviving
Trauma, Crisis & Grief

Practical & Spiritual Steps to Help
You Survive, Heal & Help Others

By Dr Michelle J. Simpson

Dedication

To the ones who have been made weak
and survived -
You are the truly strong.

Contents

Introduction

After sharing briefly and singing at a women's retreat in Arizona, USA, a young woman wanted to talk to me. 'You are not what I thought', she said. Intrigued, I also found myself inwardly preparing for the possibility of something negative. I listened as she explained.

'When I first saw you, I thought you were just a spoilt little rich girl. I thought you probably had a privileged upbringing and didn't really have many problems. I was surprised when you shared about your past and what you have been through.'

As we talked, I found out that she had also experienced a very traumatic life so far, including drugs, abuse and homelessness, and was living in a women's shelter. It was clear that her health was poor.

I was dressed down in faded jeans, a second-hand white shirt and denim waistcoat. It was creative thrift put together, nothing special, but the result was relatively trendy. My figure is good for my age. I had been at the front, singing. She put all that together, the way I looked, what I was doing, my British accent, and made a common mistake so many of us make. She judged by outward appearance and blended that judgement with a mix of her own experience and assumptions. It was only when I shared about my past that she realised how wrong her initial impression had been.

Being a 'privileged, spoilt little rich girl' is far from the truth. My parents were intelligent, well-educated, gifted and attractive people. However, they were also very broken people, their lives marred, interrupted and devastated by mistakes, loss, trouble and grief.

1

My father, an excellent sportsman, gardener, writer, and a wonderful dad in so many ways, lost a brother as a child, and his father when he was only sixteen. He married and divorced three times. Much of his life was filled with serious trouble in his relationships with his children and spouses. His second wife disappeared without a trace, never to be seen again.

My mother was a beautiful and talented woman with many awards for singing. She lost her career because of a brief affair with another man. It led to the loss of her livelihood, marriage, home and children to divorce. She married three times. Her second husband was an alcoholic. She lived with the consequences of her mistake and loss of her children her whole life. She died of lung cancer from passive smoking when she was only sixty-one.

I was the product of a non-consenting sexual encounter between parents. I lost my mother to divorce before I was four years old and lost two step mothers and step brothers after that. All through my childhood I saw my mother only once a month or once every two weeks and experienced the sense of grief and loss it caused. I witnessed violence in our home and lived with the constant threat and fear of it. I experienced sexual abuse. Because of the mess at home, my education was stunted and opportunities lost. I left home at sixteen, did jobs I didn't like just to survive, and gradually became bitter, angry and disillusioned. I was taken advantage of by men who should have known better. My mother died when I was only thirty and I had had hardly had any life with her. I have witnessed and been intimately involved in the horrors of the eating disorder, anorexia, in the life of a loved one. I have been rejected, cut off and lied about by a dear member of my own family, with the help of complete strangers.

There is much more detail and there have been more traumatic events than that, but it is enough to share for now. The purpose of this short book is not to fill your mind with the traumatised events of my own life. Nor is trauma some kind of competition to see who has been through the most awful experiences.

It's a mistake to judge by appearances. No matter what our abilities, status, influence, education, position, or appearance, trauma can come to us all. Traumatic events, crises and grief are no respecter of age, race, tribe, colour, nation, accommodation, job or religion. But as human beings, we often judge by appearances. We see only the outside, not what is happening inside and all that a person has been through. We need to understand more about a person's life and situation if we are to understand them and not form hasty opinions.

If you know someone has lived in a war-torn country, been in a persecuted minority situation, or experienced a natural disaster, bad accident or severe or sudden loss of some kind, it might be more obvious to assume the possibility that they could be suffering from trauma. However, even then you would need to find out much more to understand possible negative effects on them. Nothing can be assumed. A traumatised person could look great. They could be your colleague, your pastor, your teacher, your student, a wealthy business man, your neighbour, or your new spouse. Appearance and other factors like race, status, education and religion cannot be relied upon to gauge what a person has been through, or is going through.

Different people deal with situations differently. We can only know something has happened and its profound and negative effect on them as we spend time with people, witness and discover the *results* of trauma and grief in their lives, if we are told about their situation, or because

3

the traumatised person confides in us themselves. People can be traumatised and look and act normal, as if nothing has happened. You may well pass them in the street every day without knowing. Trauma can happen to anyone.

If you are reading this book today, perhaps you are here because you have been through a trauma that has radically affected you and altered your life. You may be in grief, afraid, in pain, and you are looking for anything that can help you through this time. Or perhaps you know someone who is suffering through trauma and its possible after-effects, and want to learn more in order to help them. Perhaps it is both of those. Whatever the reason you have started reading this book, I would like to congratulate you, not because you picked up *my* book, but because you picked up *something* to help. Congratulations because you are still alive and breathing. Congratulations for being brave, strong, determined, smart, and courageous. You may feel a long way from any of those things right now, but coming as far as you have means you have fought each day to get here and you are fighting to get to a better place. That is a tremendous achievement. Well done!

I know what that is like. On my own traumatic journey, and later experience with Complex Post Traumatic Stress Disorder, I have had to fight the daily battle of survival, hope and peace. Compounding the problems on my journey was the fact that a major family trauma happened just as I was entering menopause and experiencing challenging physical and emotional symptoms as my hormones and feelings fluctuated day and night. At the same time, I lost the use of my right arm temporarily and was in 24/7 pain. Just when I needed the most support, my husband and I experienced abuse from colleagues. Where I had managed so well the previous traumas in my life, the loss in my family was the 'last straw'. It was too much for me. So many battles at the same time made the trauma symptoms worse. I had to fight trauma on every front, emotionally, mentally, physically, and spiritually.

In the battles of my life, the injustice, tears, depression, confusion, anxiety and heartache of trauma, and the fight to live each day, I have learned some things along the way. I am not a medical doctor or mental health professional and I do not claim to be so. I am, however, a survivor. But, I'm not just a survivor. I have been able to turn my experiences to help others. At the time of writing, my loss and trauma continues. However, each day, I choose to live. I want to help you do the same. My scars, experience, along with the research and practical application I have had to do for my own survival, have given me the ability to not just understand trauma and grief, but learn how to get through it at the most real and basic level.

The reason I gave this book the title, 'Surviving Trauma, Crisis & Grief', instead of 'Healing from Trauma, Crisis and Grief, is because much of the time trauma leaves you with the feeling that you cannot and never will heal. The word 'healing' can seem huge and premature and unreasonable to someone in the depths and throes of trauma, and especially if there is significant loss or elements of the trauma are ongoing. Before we can embark on a journey called 'healing', we must first find the ways that work for us to survive from day to day. Survival is paramount. Days of survival add up and become the gradual journey towards something better that we could then call 'healing' if we wanted to. That involves practical and spiritual steps.

This book was originally written for Native Americans when we were living in Arizona on the edge of the Navaho Reservation, where serious trauma in many forms is common, but access to help and support is limited. The book is not intended to be an exhaustive or academic work. It is intended to be a genuine, practical help and a simple read using everyday language to make it easier to understand for people suffering trauma, for their helpers/carers, and for those who want to learn. Chapter Five covers the Spiritual Steps in dealing with trauma. This is written from my life as a Christian. You are invited to read this whatever your faith, or if you have no faith, but whatever, be sure to read the section called 'Forgive?' Here, the pressure to forgive is removed from the person suffering and forgiveness is placed in their control instead.

Whoever you are and whatever your belief, you are a precious human being who deserves every opportunity to reclaim their life from trauma. If you will allow me, I would like to journey with you by sharing what I have learned to help me survive and take steps into life again. My hope and earnest desire is that you will find something in this book that will help *you* survive, and find new life.

This I know for sure: YOU ARE WORTH IT.

Chapter 1

Recognising Trauma, Crisis & Grief

Firstly, I want to say how sorry I am that you have suffered trauma. No-one deserves to be traumatised by other people or devastating situations, or to go through the pain, loss and grief involved.

Perhaps no-one has ever said sorry to you or expressed their sorrow over the pain you are in from the trauma you have experienced. Sometimes, it helps to just hear someone say, 'I am *so* sorry'. There is nothing *right* about the trauma, and there is no easy, convenient, pat phrase that will make it all better. However, to hear someone say, 'I am sorry it happened and for all you are going through', and receive the love and care of that into our hearts is a good foundation on which to begin. Just pause a moment and let that seep into your heart.

Another important foundation is to understand what we are going through when we are experiencing trauma. It is harder to stand up in it all, or work towards any sense of life or healing in our soul in the midst of something we don't understand. So, let's have a look at what trauma is. As you read on you may well find words and phrases that resonate powerfully with your own feelings. This is not to create more negative emotions on the inside of you, or make you relive events. This is simply to help you come to understand, get in touch with, and identify what you are experiencing. These feelings are normal and common to those who have suffered a traumatic situation. If you have a pen or pencil, you could underline any of the words and phrases that apply to you and represent how you feel. You can use this to reassure yourself how *normal* your feelings are. Have a cup of tea or coffee with you and find a comfortable place as you read. If powerful emotions are evoked, stop, have a drink, take some deep breaths, do something else for a while, and then read on when you are ready.

This book is to help bring understanding and knowledge. With knowledge comes greater freedom. Read on knowing you are understood, that others have been there, and that you are not alone. Are you ready?

What is Trauma?

Trauma is what you experience when you are involved in or witness a deeply disturbing, distressing, or frightening event. It is an event that threatens your feelings of safety and security. It may even make you fearful for your life. It is so distressing that it profoundly marks you and affects your thinking, your behaviour, and your normal life patterns. It attacks the core of your being. It can happen to soldiers in battle. It can happen to those who witness or are involved in a murder, rape, war or natural disasters. But it can be other situations such as abandonment by a loved one, betrayal, the death of someone you are close to, a painful divorce, or violence and breakdown in your family home as a child. It is any event, or series of events, which is deeply disturbing and distressing to *you* personally.

Dr Gabor Mate states, 'Trauma is what happens inside of you as a result of traumatic events. It is a loss of connection to oneself and to the present moment.'[1] Dr Diane Langberg[2] defines trauma as a heart, mind and soul wound, which occurs when something violating, terrifying, or dehumanising has taken place.

When a person is traumatised, what they have experienced overwhelms their emotions and ability to cope. It disrupts the normal functioning of the mind and inhibits the ability to reason. It sends the brain into a process of responses from which it can find it hard to recover. It shatters beliefs and feelings of safety and security. If you have faith, what you have normally believed about God and His Word can be violently challenged. It affects physical, spiritual and emotional health and well-being. It can even make you feel that life is not worth living and bring suicidal thoughts.

What is Grief?

Grief is deep sorrow. It is especially caused by some kind of death, or a profound loss or change in some way concerning health, relationships, location and situation. Grief is a 'face' that takes the place of someone dear to you.[3] It keeps showing up, unwanted. It is unfamiliar and unfriendly and it can make you feel profoundly uncomfortable, hurt, in pain, confused, upset and frightened. It is intense emotional suffering and acute sorrow. It can leave you in shock and denial. It feels like the bottom has fallen out of your world. Raw and fragile emotions can make you think you are losing your mind. It makes you feel alone. It goes on too long, arriving in overwhelming waves that come when they choose, and the pain can be unrelenting.

Some people deny it. Some people choose not to express the grief, but their silence only covers the wounds. The wounds have no opportunity to be cleansed and heal, leading to emotional infection.[4] You fight grief, and want nothing more than the pain to leave, but it stays. You go to sleep with it, and wake to it. Fighting it is a daily, exhausting battle. You try to drown out the pain with anything that will numb it, but when the numbness wears off you are back in the same place. The only way to move forward is to learn to ride the waves of grief. You also need times when you can take a break from grief. But how do you do that? And instead of being drowned in the waves, is it possible to use them to propel you forward?

What is Crisis?

Crisis is a time of intense difficulty, trouble or danger. It is literally 'a separating', a marker, alarm moment or turning point in life.[5] It could be a short event or occur over an extended period of time. When you experience trauma, it involves a crisis of some kind. The ongoing problems caused by trauma then become part of creating a sense of ongoing crisis. Grief is often a result of a crisis in the form of a loss, intense pain over what is lost, and the further life changes and adjustments to life caused by that loss.

What is PTS?

A traumatic event can cause a person to experience severe distress both during the event and afterwards. It is called Post Traumatic Stress because the stress is caused by and continues after a traumatic event. The event may be over, but the stress continues. It is a very high degree of stress that can be very difficult to cope with. After a traumatic event, it is important to be able to receive help and support to process what happened. Early help and support can help to prevent Post Traumatic Stress becoming Post Traumatic Stress Disorder.

What is PTSD?

Post Traumatic Stress Disorder (PTSD) is what happens when trauma continues to negatively affect a person for an extended period of time. If symptoms of Post Traumatic Stress (PTS) last longer than one to three months, you may have PTSD (opinions vary on the timeframe used for diagnosis). The brain processes become stuck, disabling them from being able to process the event in a healing way.

A person can become 'stuck' in a place of grief, shock and anxiety over a traumatic event. They cannot seem to get past it. The event plays over and over in their mind, no matter how they try to stop it. They are plagued with invasive thoughts and images of what happened. Anxiety and fear is triggered by anything that reminds them of the trauma, and even by things that are unrelated and yet stir memories such as certain smells or sounds, atmospheres, words or other sensory stimulation. They try to avoid anything that relates to the traumatic event in any way. PTSD is a psychological injury. PTSD often presents in the following ways:[6]

Re-experiencing symptoms: During re-experiencing symptoms, the person relives the event in some way. They may have:

- Flashbacks – reliving the trauma over and over, including physical symptoms like a racing heart or sweating
- Bad dreams
- Frightening thoughts

These symptoms may cause problems in your everyday routines and can start from your own thoughts and feelings. Words, objects, or situations that are reminders of the traumatic event can also trigger '*re-experiencing*' symptoms.

Avoidance symptoms:

- Staying away from places, events, or objects that are reminders of the experience
- Avoiding thoughts or feelings related to the traumatic event

Things or situations that remind a person of the traumatic event can trigger avoidance symptoms. These symptoms may cause a person to change his or her personal routine. For example, after a bad car accident, a person who usually drives may avoid driving or riding in a car.

Arousal and reactivity symptoms:

- Being easily startled
- Feeling tense or 'on edge'
- Having difficulty sleeping and/or having angry outbursts

Trauma can leave certain parts of the brain in a state of hyper-vigilance or 'arousal'. Instead of just being triggered by something that brings back memories of the traumatic event, arousal symptoms are usually constant, putting the person continuously 'on guard' to an abnormal degree. This can make the person feel afraid, stressed and angry. They live in a state of fight or flight and can be very sensitive to the smallest triggers. These symptoms may make it hard to do daily tasks such as sleeping, eating, or concentrating.

Cognition and mood symptoms:

- Trouble remembering key features of the traumatic event

- Negative thoughts about oneself or the world
- Distorted feelings like guilt or blame
- Loss of interest in enjoyable activities

Cognition and mood symptoms can begin or worsen after the traumatic event. These symptoms can make the person feel alienated or detached from friends or family members.

Diagnosing PTSD

To be diagnosed with PTSD, an adult must have all of the following for at least one month:
- At least one re-experiencing symptom
- At least one avoidance symptom
- At least two arousal and reactivity symptoms
- At least two cognition and mood symptoms.[7]

What Traumas Cause PTSD?

There are conflicting opinions over what constitutes a traumatic event that could lead to PTSD. For many years, it has been limited to things like soldiers fighting in battles and witnessing horrific deaths, losing limbs in accidents or war, people being raped, violent attacks, kidnapping, natural disasters, or witnessing any of these events. It did not include traumatic events like a child going through their parents' divorce, being abandoned by someone close etc. Now, however, this thinking is changing and any frightening, disturbing or distressing event that threatens feelings of safety and security can be considered applicable.

Early traumas in childhood, can lead to a greater possibility of traumatic events later in life turning into PTSD. This means that a person's vulnerability to getting

PTSD can, in part, also depend on their early life experiences and their consequent ability to cope with further trauma in adulthood.

People are Different

People are different. One person might go through a traumatic event and recover while another person might go through the same traumatic event and go on to experience PTSD. Much depends on:

- early life experiences,
- how much trauma a person has already been through and their available coping capacity,
- what they are dealing with when a trauma occurs,
- how sensitive they are to a particular type of traumatic event depending on its relationship to them and their previous experience,
- their personality and whether they are more vulnerable to anxiety, depression, fear etc.

Research indicates that soldiers who experienced trauma in childhood (pre-war vulnerability) are more likely to experience PTSD in severe war combat situations, than soldiers who did not experience childhood trauma.[8] Trauma may lead to PTSD in children where emotions and understanding are less developed and they are frightened. Whether or not a person gets PTSD could also depend on how much help they received to recover from original trauma and the degree to which that was successful.

We cannot say that someone should not be affected by PTSD because another person involved in the same traumatic event did not get PTSD. Nor can we say that a person 'should not' have PTSD because the traumatic event they went through was 'not traumatic enough' to affect them. People are not the same and events affect them differently.

A particular set of factors will be in place for a particular person to get PTSD, but all of them will come together and be sparked by a certain traumatic event/s they witnessed or in which they were involved.

What is Complex Trauma?

Complex Trauma, or Complex Post Traumatic Stress Disorder, is often written as CPTSD, C-PTSD or Complex PTSD. C-PTSD has been described by psychologist and trauma expert Dr Christine Courtois as 'a type of trauma that occurs repeatedly and cumulatively, usually over a period of time and within specific relationships and contexts.'[9] Examples would include severe child abuse, domestic abuse, or multiple military deployments into dangerous locales.

MIND, a UK mental health charity, describes the following types of traumatic events as possible causes for Complex PTSD:

- childhood abuse

- neglect or abandonment

- ongoing domestic violence or abuse

- repeatedly witnessing violence or abuse

- being forced to become a sex worker

- torture

- kidnapping or slavery

- being a prisoner of war.

The chances of developing C-PTSD are more likely if you have experienced the following:

- trauma at an early age

- long-lasting trauma

- escape or rescue were unlikely or impossible

- multiple traumas.

In her article "Complex Trauma, Complex Reactions: Assessment and Treatment", Dr Christine Courtois lists symptoms of Complex PTSD (C-PTSD) as including difficulty regulating affective impulses such as anger and self-destructiveness, dissociative episodes, a chronic sense of guilt or responsibility, difficulty trusting people or feeling intimate, hopelessness or despair, and other somatic (physical) or medical problems. Individuals who have been traumatized repeatedly over a period of time or within specific settings and scenarios are vulnerable to many of these emotional struggles.

Regardless of the degree of trauma suffered, the important thing to realize is that help is available, even for those who have survived the most excruciating situations.[10]

Spiritual Trauma & Abuse

To finish this chapter I want to highlight another kind of trauma which has its own particular characteristics.

Churches and faith communities are meant to be safe places where spiritual leaders help empower people in their lives and spheres of influence. Sadly, this is not always as it should be. Sometimes leaders misuse their position and use spiritual authority to control, manipulate or shame people into certain behaviours or ways of thinking. Often this is due to incorrect or extreme interpretations of scripture, or due to wrong teaching they have themselves received. As a result, people find themselves trapped in a system, feeling abused by a leader, and living to a standard of performance that saps true spiritual life and can leave them feeling guilty and traumatised.

Spiritual trauma can occur from abuse experienced in a spiritual or church context, in any kind of ministry context, from any kind of religious abuse in the name of 'God', when people seek to get something from others through coercion and control, or to exert power over them. This can be done through the erroneous use of scripture to add a 'divine spin' that forces people into doing what they are told. They may be led to believe that they are 'disobeying' God or being rebellious if they don't. Abuse may be the result of a culture of wrong treatment at the hands of another believer. Spiritual trauma can create guilt, shame, fear, confusion, disillusionment, anger, and also lead to PTSD.

Chapter 2

Don't Worry. It's Normal

It is very important for you to know that if you are suffering the effects of trauma, grief, PTS, PTSD, or C-PTSD, you are not weak or strange. You are human. If you have experienced trauma, you have suffered a psychological injury. If this injury was on the outside of your body, a broken limb, or a big, noticeable wound, everyone could see it and understand why you are in pain. Because it is inside, people don't see the injury, and neither do you. But *you* feel the effects of the injury. You feel the damage and pain. Sometimes, these kinds of injuries don't receive the help or treatment they need because an invisible injury is often ignored. However the *effects* of the injury are very noticeable to you and those involved in your life.

The Effects of Trauma

Trauma and grief can affect a person emotionally, mentally, physically, socially and spiritually. To help you understand some of the feelings and other effects of trauma, here is a list of words I comprised from my own experience, and learning of others' experiences, that you might be able to identify with. I didn't compile this list to make you feel more miserable but to give you something to relate to, to see that different people experience a variety of different emotions, and yet the same kind of emotions are normal to anyone suffering trauma and grief. You may also experience change from one of these emotions to another several times in one day. You may even be able to add your own words to this list:

Emotional: depression, anger and angry outbursts, pointlessness, irritability, impatience, up and  down feelings, suicidal thoughts and feelings, sadness, hatred, unforgiveness, revenge, disillusionment, loss of purpose, fear, terror, confusion, shock, despair, grief, disgust, aggression, less capacity to cope with further stress, loss of trust, anxiety, alarm, desolation, agony, sense of betrayal, sense of injustice, frequent crying, hopelessness, numbness, loss of enjoyment in what was previously enjoyed, loss of confidence, emotional fatigue, out of control, hypersensitivity to triggers that relate to the incident *and* that don't relate to the incident, fear that this will be for the rest of your life.

Mental: a feeling of being stuck in your thinking, inability to move away from certain thoughts,  intrusive thoughts, repetitive thoughts that loop around and around, replaying the event, disturbed dreams/nightmares, inability to function at some mental level, loss of focus, confusion, distracted, need for greater stimulation and distraction, forgetfulness, putting oneself down in thought and word/berating self, slower thinking, lessened capacity to make decisions, flashbacks, like you are going crazy, can't shake it off, mental shutdown.

Physical: lethargy, slowness, tiredness, fatigue, exhaustion, headaches/migraines, nervous habits such as nail biting, pacing, rocking, panic attacks, intense pain in gut/heart, feeling of intense 'butterflies' in stomach/heart, waves of grief, discomfort, illness, stress symptoms such as spots/poor skin/dull eyes, shaking, hearing things, lessened physical ability, reduced energy, weight gain or weight loss, increased or decreased appetite, suicide attempts, unusual behaviour, comfort eating/starving, reduced ability to function normally in life, heart palpitations, hyperactivity, weakness, unexplained aches and pains, loss of libido, miscarriage, adrenaline rushes, dependencies and addictions.

Social: isolation, desire to shut self away from people and life, not talking, crying or depressed when with people, unhappy around happy people, feeling others don't understand, angry with others, blaming, further hurt due to insensitive/ unhelpful/inappropriate responses from others, loss of enjoyment used to have in relationships and social activities, marriage problems, separation, divorce, increased family stress, loss of trust in people.

Spiritual: feelings of being lost, abandonment by God, loss of faith, loss of trust, feeling unprotected by God, doubting His goodness/Word/existence/call, doubting your salvation, loss of vision and purpose, loss of spiritual energy, loss of desire to serve Him, inability to continue in ministry,

disillusionment, anger towards God, turning away from God/church/other believers, no desire to read or hear His Word, spiritual things become hard to take in, struggling with forgiveness and burdened with further guilt after you have forgiven but still experience pain and anger, feeling that God expects too much, feeling the enemy is greater than God, questions of 'Why?', feelings of injustice, feeling 'at sea', unanchored and lost, hardening your heart to survive, overwhelmed, crying in church gatherings, feeling like an atheist/backslider, grieving loss of relationship with God and loss of His presence, fighting to hold on to faith and feeling like failing at it, made worse by happy people around you, won't or can't praise or worship, hard to pray, feeling God is not hearing/answering/speaking/helping/there, feeling of betrayal and being let down.

Naturally, when any kind of trauma occurs, not just spiritual, your spiritual world and beliefs can also be traumatised. As people typically attribute God with ultimate power and ability, they also attribute Him with the ultimate responsibility for what happens to them. In other words, when something really bad happens, there is a tendency for some people to blame God and to view God as uncaring and non-compassionate. It's even possible that God might be seen in the same light as the perpetrators of the trauma.

In trauma, feelings of anger towards God are normal. It doesn't mean that you are correct in what you think about God in your anger, but the nature of trauma can deeply disturb a person's spiritual equilibrium.

The Effect of Trauma on the Brain

Our experiences affect the development of our brain from childhood. As billions of brain cells, or neurons, communicate with each other by sending electrical signals, they form the foundational architecture of the child's brain during this important developmental period. A child's experiences during the earliest years of life have a lasting impact on that architecture of the developing brain. Positive experiences are needed for the formation of healthy brain architecture including appropriate input from responsive and stable relationships with caring adults. Without this positive stimulation to the senses and emotions, the brain will instead be impacted by potentially harmful stress hormones.[11]

The brain continues to be impacted by experiences into adulthood. Like falling over and banging yourself can break the skin and cause bleeding, or cause a broken bone, traumatic events have the ability to negatively affect the normal functioning of the brain. Brain scans on people who have suffered trauma have revealed that the trauma has caused the brain to function differently.[12]

To put it simply, the brain works by millions and millions of connections across and along nerve pathways. In trauma, these pathways stop working the same way. The pathways are changed.

The temporal and frontal lobes regulate emotions, especially fear, and deal with memory, planning, organising, judgment, logic and decision-making. These shut down and become inactive, almost asleep. This makes it hard to focus and causes poor memory, poor judgment, little ability to plan, and no joy.

Meanwhile, the motor areas in the lower part of the brain go into overdrive! They coordinate the active parts of the body such as limbs and eyes. They become over-reactive and create hypersensitivity to stressors and triggers which may even have nothing to do with the original event. They cause your natural survival instincts such as the 'fight, freeze or flight response' to kick in. This increased functioning causes a greater level of stress chemicals (adrenaline and cortisol) to be released in your body, leaving you in a state of hyper-arousal, ready to fight back, feeling frozen and helpless, or wanting to run away fast to protect yourself. This effect on your brain does not mean you are going mad or crazy. Your brain is trying to deal with the trauma and find ways to process it and respond to it, but with the areas of the brain that deal with reasoning and judgment having shut down from the trauma, this is more difficult to do.

Memories and emotions, especially traumatic ones, are stored in the brain and certain triggers reactivate these memories and emotions, bringing the fear and pain alive again even long after the event has happened.

History and Personality

As I said earlier, trauma affects people differently. If you have a history of traumatic events, a major incident in your past, traumas or abuse in childhood, you will possibly respond to further trauma in life less well than those who have not had those events happen in the past. Previous traumas, especially in childhood, can reduce the capacity of the brain and body to cope with further traumas. This is not your fault. It is not a weakness on your part. It's not because of something you have done wrong.

To give you a picture, it is simply that you live with an emotional and physical 'cup' that is more full from previous traumas than the physical and emotional cup of someone who has not had so much trauma. Every day stressors that are added increase your stress levels closer to the rim of the cup. Any further traumatic event added to that causes your stress levels to overflow. The stress goes beyond your capacity to contain it.[13]

This will not happen to everyone. My husband's and my response to a traumatic event in our family were quite different. While he was understandably in great pain over the loss, he coped better than me. He did not suffer the same symptoms as me. He could get on with things in life without interference from intrusive and invasive thoughts. Conversely, I suffered many symptoms of grief, trauma and PTSD. What are the differences between us?

- He is a man and I am a woman. Obviously, that can make some difference. The male brain can have the ability to put events into different 'compartments' of life more easily. He has the ability to 'process' things out. A woman's brain revolves much more around relationships. If there is a trauma in an important relationship, her response may be different. She may experience a greater variety of emotions far more intensely. If a child is involved, a mother's heart can feel things much more intensely too. This is a generalisation of course, and many men and women may respond differently to the above. However, research is showing that women are more prone to PTSD due to the combination of the greater amount of emotion they experience in a trauma situation, and the greater chance of having been previously traumatised. The nature of the traumas they experience such as sexual abuse, means women are more than twice as likely to get PTSD than men.[14]

- His personality is different. My husband naturally has a more easy-going, accepting attitude to life. That doesn't mean he likes every situation or doesn't want to change things. It doesn't mean he doesn't feel the pain of situations. But a more easy-going personality may feel less anxious and stressed by an event.

- He does not have a history of trauma. My husband comes from a family of faith with no history of divorce, violence or extreme trauma. He lived in the same house until the age of eighteen, had mostly positive experiences, good friends, extended family of faith, steady relationships, a church social life, parents who stayed in the area of his birth, steady education which led to a degree and an excellent job offer. It wasn't perfect but it was not trauma-filled.

By contrast, my family was very broken, I witnessed violent threats, was exposed to constant fear of aggression and trouble at home, and experienced underage sexual abuse. I was unhappy through much of my schooling, drank and smoked, played truant, and ran away from home twice. I lost my mother early to lung cancer, had a major accident requiring three surgeries and three years of recovery, had a chronic illness for many years, and have had forty homes.

I need to mention here that I have had lots of positive experiences as well, but I share this with you to show you the difference between people and their history of life experiences, personality, and potential coping capacity from those early experiences. Those who have suffered more, earlier in life, may be more susceptible to a traumatic event turning into Post Traumatic Stress, Post Traumatic Stress Disorder, or Complex Post Traumatic Stress Disorder. If soldiers who have had previously traumatic experiences in war, or as children, are more prone to Post Traumatic Stress Disorder on experiencing further traumatic incidents, then it makes sense not just for soldiers in battle, but for people in the battles and traumas of life.[15]

Tendency to Catastrophise

When a person has suffered trauma or a multitude of traumas, they can develop the tendency to 'catastrophise'. That means when future difficult situations arise, they may experience those situations as more 'catastrophic' than they actually are, or as more catastrophic than others see them. This isn't surprising.

When trauma has filled your 'capacity' to cope, you can become so used to negative and bad things happening that you begin to expect negative and bad things to happen. You start to believe the worst and see the worst scenarios in your mind when they have not even happened. This is irrational at the best of times, but trauma can cause distorted new patterns of thinking that can become difficult to control. It is like a rut, a default negative thinking pattern, a ditch that your mind falls into due to a 're-wiring' that has taken place because of trauma.

Depression & Anxiety

Because trauma can rock and change our world so violently and cause us to view all of life differently, we can find ourselves grasping for anything that might feel familiar or comfortable. It's frightening to discover that nothing feels familiar or comfortable in the way it used to. The body now has to cope with frequent surges of pain, grief, and releases of adrenaline and cortisol. This is exhausting mentally, emotionally, and physically.

A traumatic event may have also caused a long-term or permanent change in our circumstances which can be extremely difficult to adjust to. This combination of stressors on the body can lead to a chemical shift resulting in long-term depression. Fear of the massive amount of change, and fear that a situation may not change, that your life will never be the same, and fear of further trauma can create a hypersensitivity on the inside of you, leading to greater anxiety about life in general. This can lead to a condition called Generalised Anxiety Disorder (GAD).

Shock

A traumatic event or situation usually comes as a shock. Just as a serious physical accident can create a risk of the person going into shock, shock to our emotions can be just as dangerous. Even smaller, brief shocks like a near-miss car accident, or someone creeping up on us and suddenly surprising us, can cause a fright, a racing heart, and the need to calm down. Really shocking situations, however, are not always easily shaken off or made better by a cup of tea. Real shock can lodge itself in your psyche and remain there so that you live in an extended state of shock. This shock is renewed every time you recall the event which may, especially initially, be many times day and night. When we say something is 'a shock to the system', that is exactly what it means. It is a shock that disrupts our systems physically, emotionally, and in every other way. Unable to make sense of it, the brain keeps trying to get hold of it, process it, and put it into a suitable box or file, but cannot find one. This inability to find an appropriate place for the event, or an effective response to it, leaves a person feeling in an almost continuous state of shock.

An Important Step

Understanding what has happened to you and why you feel the way you do is an important step in surviving and regaining your life. None of this is your fault. It is simply the way the brain and body respond to a large and overwhelming degree of trauma. Recognising it, understanding it, and understanding ourselves, can help us to survive in our journey of healing.

You are not going crazy. You are a person who has experienced a shocking, traumatic event and crazy circumstances. Your response is normal. You are not weak. You are not unspiritual. You do not need to feel guilty. If you are a person of faith, God is not angry with you because of what you are going through. You are a soldier wounded on the battlefield of life and experiencing the deep pain of that wound.

Is there hope? Yes. Like the rainbow was originally intended as a sign of peace and shows us the presence of sunshine in rain, there is hope, and the real possibility that colour can be restored in your world.

In spite of the injury you have received and negative altered pathways that have been created, your brain is the most amazing creation. It has an ability called 'neuroplasticity'.[16] That means the nerve pathways affected and created negatively by the trauma can be *reformed*, whatever age you are. New positive pathways can be formed again. That means recovery is possible.

Part of that journey towards recovery and life is knowing that you are normal, and that you are not alone. You are in good company.

Chapter 3

In Good Company

You have company in your pain. Feeling alone at a traumatic time can make everything feel worse than it does already. Even if you feel alone, or friendless or far from family, it helps to know you are not alone in your experience and feelings. There are many who have walked or are walking this path in our world today, and who have walked it throughout history.

Grief and trauma, simply because of their nature, cause us to put much of our focus and attention on ourselves. This is not surprising or wrong. It is necessary and unavoidable. It is a very intense way to live, however, and can be utterly exhausting.

In the midst of our pain, it can help to get our eyes off ourselves for a while and look at someone else's life. Seeing where others have been can help us put things in perspective, at least for a period of time, and make us feel less alone. There are many around us who are experiencing trauma right now. You will know others in your own family or circle of friends or acquaintances who have suffered something traumatic. News on the internet, TV and radio from around the world is full of it. There are many accounts and modern-day stories of people dealing with traumas, including refugees of war-torn countries and victims of all kinds of atrocities. In our own circle of friends and contacts we know of three suicides. But my goal here is not to fill your mind with details of these. You don't need that. So I have chosen to share stories with you that at least put a little more distance between you and the events, the distance of time.

Trauma is not new. It is 'as old as the hills' or at least as old as man himself. That gives me the opportunity to share with you true accounts from a much older story book.

Whether you are a believer in God or some other kind of faith or not, the Bible is both an ancient and accurate book, and the best-selling, most widely read book in the world. It's also an excellent source of accounts that show us how people have been affected by trauma since the earliest times. Let's take a look at some of those people who suffered trauma and see some of the circumstances and feelings involved. You might be able to relate in some way. We will also see how these people came through and how they might offer us hope in our pain.

The First Family

The earliest biblical record of trauma is the self-inflicted one caused by the first recorded people, Adam and Eve. They were created to prosper in the environment of a beautiful garden with a life of goodness prepared for them. They were totally at peace in an idyllic setting where there were no problems, all their needs were met, they knew God as their Creator and Father, and knew only harmony and well-being. There was only one thing in the garden they were instructed to avoid. For the sake of their own well-being, they were given a clear warning not to eat from the Tree of the Knowledge of Good and Evil. However, beguiled by temptation and the look of the fruit, Eve handed some of it to Adam, and they both ate. In the moments that followed, everything changed. They suddenly became aware of shame and fear, and their wilful wrongdoing separated them from God and His goodness and put them into the cold, harsh realities of a fallen world.

Trauma had begun and its tentacles would now begin their reach through the generations.

In the next traumatic event recorded in their lives, their own son picks up a stone and in intense jealousy, hits his brother over the head and murders him. Adam and Eve's own disobedience and foolishness had lost them their perfect world, their home, their peace of mind, their relationship with God, and their own child. On top of that they suffered the guilt of knowing it was their own fault.

However, trauma doesn't have to end that way. It doesn't have to have the last say. In the very first traumatic incident of paradise being lost, we see God providing a solution for us all; a way back to a relationship with Him through His Son, Jesus. Jesus' death on the Cross and resurrection, and the shedding of His own blood for us purchases forgiveness for sin and our eternal salvation.

Some traumas like the murder of Abel by his brother, Cain, the loss of a child, have no solutions. Abel could not be brought back to them. But there was a 'compensation'. Seth was born. Joy was restored to Adam and Eve through the birth of Seth (a Hebrew name meaning 'compensation'). Seth's genealogy eventually led to the birth of Christ. Sometimes, in the event of loss and trauma, we must look for what might be a 'compensation'.

Joseph

Joseph grew up with eight half-brothers and one younger brother, Benjamin, in a family that loved and revered God. His father, Jacob, expressed his love and preference for Joseph openly and this made the half-brothers jealous. It was the last straw when Joseph told them of his dreams about becoming great and his family bowing down to him. Whatever the family dynamics and personal mistakes, Joseph did not deserve what happened next. At just age seventeen, he was thrown into a pit by his brothers who were eager for revenge. He was given no water and he could not escape. They would not let him out despite his cries and pleading.

If Joseph was afraid then, things were about to get much worse. Heartlessly, his brothers sold him as a slave to passing slave traders. He was, in modern terms, trafficked by his brothers. He was dragged across Egypt, probably on foot, for about two hundred miles over fifteen days. When he arrived, he was stripped of all he knew, dressed in different clothes, given food he was not used to, expected to respond to a language he did not understand, and set to work as a slave.

Joseph was in shock. We can imagine that he was exhausted, frightened, suffering culture-shock, and the sudden wrenching from his beloved family and all that was familiar. He was experiencing intense grief, anger and confusion over his betrayal, and fear over his future. Would he ever see his father and mother again? What about his younger brother, Benjamin? His world was reeling from trauma.

Joseph was made a slave to Potiphar, captain of the palace guard. Just as he was trying to live with the mind-blowing adjustment necessary to do this job, another traumatic event occurred. Potiphar's wife was attracted to Joseph and tried to seduce him. When he, in his integrity towards himself, God and Potiphar, rejected her advances, she screamed for the guards and lied about him, telling the guards and Potiphar that he tried to force her to have sex with him. Fortunate to keep his life, Joseph was thrown into prison. As the door locked behind him and yet more of his freedom was taken away, the injustice must have been overwhelming. What did he think? What had he done wrong? Was he going to die? Where was God? Why had He allowed this chain of traumatic events to happen?

While most prisoners were there just waiting to see if they would be executed, somehow Joseph managed to hold on to his faith in God and become useful. The Bible doesn't give us any of the details about his emotions and struggle, but being human like us we only have to use our imagination to understand the pain and confusion he was in. The Bible does describe, however, how Joseph used his gifts and talents in the prison. What else did he have? Stripped of his family, language, culture, home, love, and freedom, he employed what he had left – his talents. It kept him busy, kept his mind occupied, and helped him survive. He applied himself to whatever he could do with excellence. His abilities impressed the prison warden and he was given charge over the other prisoners. He also helped two fellow inmates, correctly interpreting the dreams of a butler and a baker. Just as Joseph had interpreted, the baker was executed but the butler was freed. Joseph asked the butler to remember him when he returned to his role for Pharaoh (Egypt's monarch). However, the butler forgot and Joseph was let down once again.

Finally, Pharaoh had a disturbing dream that needed interpretation and became desperate for help. At that point, the butler remembered Joseph and told Pharaoh about him. Joseph was released to interpret the dream for Pharaoh regarding a future famine in Egypt. Joseph was then promoted to governor, a position just below Pharaoh himself, and given the role of overseeing the distribution of food in the coming famine. His life was reversed from tragedy and trauma to triumph.

When his half-brothers arrived in Egypt to buy food during the famine, Joseph recognised them although *they* did not recognise Joseph. Joseph had to work through some powerful emotions. After all that had been done to him, the memory of that pit, and the terrible betrayal of being sold, the images flooded back to his mind. His heart raced as the pain was triggered in his soul. Eventually revealing his identity, he extended love to his brothers. His position enabled him to care for and save his own family from starvation in the years to come.

Joseph was given a new beginning and his family were saved, but he had to travel the journey of his own grief, shock and pain to get there. He obviously kept busy. He did his best. He kept living what he could in the circumstances. Where did he find the inner resources to hold on in the face of such grief and trauma? Joseph had the advantage of youthful vigour and vision, but he also had a faith that upheld and strengthened him from within. Also, God had a plan for his life. In this case, it was the saving of his entire family and a whole nation.

Somewhere in the trauma, while it can be almost impossible to see at the time, perhaps there can also be the unfolding of an unexpected plan.

Jacob

While most people focus on what happens to Joseph in this ancient and yet modern and relevant story of human trafficking, the trauma the parents suffered is often only given a brief glance by comparison. But Jacob and his wife, Rachel, suffered one of the worst traumas. They lost a child. They believed Joseph to be dead. Joseph and Benjamin were the only two children from their union and to lose their beloved Joseph was a massive shock which changed their whole lives.

On top of the loss, the manner of it horrified them. Afraid to tell their parents what they had really done to Joseph, the half-brothers daubed the special coat his father had made for him in animal blood and told Jacob and

Rachel that Joseph had been torn apart by wild animals. What an awful image to have in their minds.

During those years of grief and loss, Jacob also lost his beloved wife Rachel, who never saw her son Joseph again. Their hearts had been broken, Jacob's twice over, and now he faced the perils of a terrible famine.

During the famine, all the brothers except Benjamin, travelled to Egypt to ask for grain. After losing his son, Joseph, Jacob kept Benjamin safely by his side. The rest of the brothers did not realise on arrival that the powerful man responsible for food distribution was Joseph himself! Shocked to see his brothers, Joseph did not give away his identity. Instead, longing to see his younger brother Benjamin again, Joseph came up with a clever plan. He accused his brothers of being spies and confined his half-brother, Simeon, in jail. Joseph tricked the remaining brothers into returning home and proving their identity and innocence by bringing Benjamin back to Egypt with them. When they told their father that Benjamin had to go to Egypt, Jacob, he was terrified! He cried out, 'Joseph is no more and Simeon is no more, and now you want to take Benjamin. Everything is against me!'[17]

Here we see Jacob responding with a case of 'catastrophising' and no wonder! He believes he has lost two sons already. He is rightly concerned for Benjamin's safety and afraid he might lose him too. The trauma and his grief cause him to believe that 'everything' is against him and everything will go wrong. And who can blame him? This is a normal response in the traumatised person. In the end, Joseph revealed his identity. Jacob and his entire household were invited to live in Goshen where Joseph and his family lived, and were saved from the ravages of famine. Jacob was protected, loved and surrounded by his family in old age.

Is it really possible that something good could come out of things that are so bad? Is there a possibility that something good could come out of the terrible trauma you have experienced?

Let's look at one more person.

Naomi

Naomi was displaced from her home in Bethlehem by the ravages of famine and went with her husband to the land of Moab. Perhaps there she could make a new life and find greater security for her two sons?

However, some time after arriving, Naomi's husband died. In grief, Naomi was left with two sons, both of whom were not well. One was called Mahlon which means *sickly*, and the other she called Chilion which means *wasting and decay*. Both sons grew old enough to marry women from Moab, but then ten years later both sons died. What a tragedy! The land of Moab, the place in which they had hoped to find a better life as a family had left her with nothing but loss, tragedy, and traumatic memories.

Grasping for something steady and familiar in a sea of turmoil, Naomi decided to return to Bethlehem, the land of her family. All she had left were her two daughters-in-law. One decided to stay and continue with life in Moab. The other daughter-in-law, Ruth, loved Naomi and would not leave her. Together they went to Bethlehem. There, Naomi had to start life all over again. People and things in the city had changed and she had missed many important events. She had no income, no security for her old age, and she was bearing the grief of loss, quite possibly for the rest of her life.

For Naomi, life lost its purpose. Grief and trauma made her feel worthless, forgotten, abandoned and hopeless. She lost her belief in God's love for her. She told people to stop calling her Naomi (beautiful grace of God) and to call her *Mara* instead (meaning bitterness). She said of God, "I went out full, and the Lord has brought me home again empty."

However, while all seemed lost, Naomi had two small but powerful abilities working in her favour. Firstly, she was a shrewd woman who understood the culture of her day and how to work with it. Secondly, while life had not worked out as she would have wanted, she was a good mother and a kind-hearted woman who cared about her daughter-in-law and wanted to help life work out for her. She sent Ruth to work in the fields of her wealthy relative and land owner, Boaz. Ruth was given work gleaning the remains of the harvest. Boaz favoured Ruth by telling the other workers to leave more stalks of grain to fall for her to take home to Naomi. Boaz had clearly shown a liking for Ruth. Naomi told Ruth what to do to win the hand of this influential next-of-kin. Ruth took her mother-in-law's advice and Boaz and Ruth got married and had a child.

How things changed! Naomi was provided for, became a nurse for her new grandson, had a grandchild on which to lavish her affection and teach about life and God, and was a mother and a mentor for Ruth. On top of that, her grandson, Obed, became the grandfather to David, the shepherd boy who became the king of Israel, whose psalms in the Bible have been and still are such a source of comfort, strength and encouragement to so many over centuries.

As Naomi looked out for her daughter-in-law, she ended up being looked out for by God and others. It was a different life to the one Naomi had expected, but as she used the seemingly small gifts and abilities she had available, new opportunities and possibilities arose for her and Ruth, and Naomi was gradually able to regain some life and move forward to a better place.

Some of the bravest people in our world are those who look out for others in the midst of their own pain and trauma. Perhaps, even in your trauma, you will discover you have gifts and abilities that will be a blessing to you and others, and help *you* regain some life too.

Choose to Keep Living

All of the feelings that Joseph and Naomi would have gone through were normal in their situations. They went through their own personal 'hells'. Their feelings were not surprising. Neither are yours.

The thing I noticed about Joseph, Jacob, and Naomi was that despite the trauma they experienced and their world collapsing, they chose to keep living. The burden of their grief was overwhelming. Joseph suffered terrible injustice and the pain of betrayal. Naomi's grief was so huge that, while she did not lose her belief in God's existence, she lost belief in His love and care for her, lost sight of her own worth, and lost hope for her future. There would have been times she wondered if it was worth living.

But Joseph, Jacob, and Naomi all chose to keep living. They put one foot in front of the other and did what they could. Through the pain, through the grief, they chose life. Joseph did what he could, walking in integrity, making himself useful and using his gifts and skills in the prison. Jacob kept going in spite of loss and was rewarded with being united once more with his son and provision for the family. Naomi, even in her grief, loss of trust in God, and loss of confidence in her own worth, made a decision to do something, to return to her homeland to be with her relatives, and advised her daughter-in-law Ruth in matters concerning Boaz.

While life turned out differently to what they thought, each of them came out to a place of new hope, new purpose, new life, and new beginnings.

I am not saying that it is easy. I am not saying that the pain disappears because of new circumstances. I know the debilitating pain and depression of trauma, the loss, the numbness, the grief, and the daily battle. I do not minimize the difficulty one bit. It is a daily decision to live, where big achievements give way to small ones, and sometimes it feels like none at all. Each day is a step. Sometimes it feels like you make a step forward and then a step back. But each day and each moment you choose life, you gradually discover a new life which helps you cope better.

Somehow, if we will keep walking, even if it feels like stumbling along, doing what we can, we will discover a new place too. The time that takes and the manner of the journey will be different for everyone. If your best right now is to eat properly, get out of bed and get dressed, or feed the dog, buy food or water the plants, do what you can. If your best right now is to get up and get to work, like Joseph and Naomi, do what you can and do the best you can do. Keep living. Every step matters, no matter how small it may seem. Everything you do counts. You might feel alone, but you are not. And while it may seem impossible and a million miles away, somewhere in the mess and morass that feels like your mind and life right now, there can be a compensation, an unexpected plan, and though hard to believe, something good. You may even come through this being a blessing to others and blessing yourself in ways you never imagined.

There is no-one yet who has been able to prevent the rainbow's colours in glints of sunlight appearing after the rain.

In Good Company

THE

PRACTICAL

STEPS

Chapter 4

Practical Steps to Survive the Journey towards Healing

We've seen how trauma has affected people from the earliest time. We know from the ancient and modern experiences of others that you are not alone. But now, let's focus on you. Yes, you. You matter.

What you have experienced may have torn at your self-esteem, your confidence and your feelings of worth and value as a person. Perhaps it has made life feel like it is not worth living.

But life is worth it. You are worth it. Your presence and contribution are worth it. Your gifts, talents, abilities, love, and personality are worth it. You are needed.

Trauma wants to steal the sense of worth and value from you. Now is the time, more than ever in your life, to care for yourself, to nurture and to regain your sense of worth and value, not just to the same level as before, but to an even greater level. To do this, you need to do good things for yourself, to nurture *you*.

The following practical steps can help you to provide the care you need for yourself, or for others. Self-care is vital when dealing with trauma.

Professional Care

Firstly, I want to say that the following steps in the next section on self care are not to keep you from seeking help and treatment from a medical or mental health professional. Early care for trauma can help to prevent trauma from turning into Post Traumatic Stress Disorder (PTSD).

If you are diagnosed with PTS, PTSD, or C-PTSD, there is treatment available such as counselling, Cognitive Behavioural Therapy (CBT) and other cognitive therapies, Eye Movement Desensitization & Reprocessing (EMDR), and others.   Medication can be used for associated symptoms such as depression or anxiety.

When seeking help, ask your doctor for a referral for trauma counselling and treatment or look for private care. Check that you are referred to someone who specialises in treating trauma, Post Traumatic Stress Disorder, and Complex Trauma.   They must be professionals with whom you feel safe and comfortable.

It is important that you see someone who knows the difference between PTS, PTSD and Complex PTSD (C-PTSD) and knows what they are doing. You should check that any expert you are referred to does not place an expectation on you to recover from PTSD or C-PTSD in a certain period of time. There can be no time frame. It is not possible to make that guarantee. Everyone is different and the effects of trauma and PTSD remain with people differently. They should also understand the difference between Post Traumatic Stress Disorder, Complex Post Traumatic Stress Disorder, and Borderline Personality Disorder (recently been renamed in the UK as Emotionally Unstable Personality Disorder), so you are not misdiagnosed.

Cognitive Behavioural Therapy (CBT)

The Mayo Clinic describes Cognitive Behavioural Therapy as:

'a common type of talk therapy (psychotherapy)...with a mental health counsellor (psychotherapist or therapist) in a structured way, attending a limited number of sessions. CBT helps you become aware of inaccurate or negative thinking so you can view challenging situations more clearly and respond to them in a more effective way.'[18]

In combination with other therapies or by itself, CBT can be an effective tool in treating mental health disorders such as depression and PTSD, OCD (Obsessive Compulsive Disorder) and eating disorders. It can also help people manage anxiety, cope with grief and loss, manage stressful life situations, cope with illness, overcome emotional trauma related to abuse or violence, identify emotions, and resolve relational conflicts.

It is often used in conjunction with an anti-depressant medication.

Eye Movement Desensitisation and Reprocessing (EMDR)

WebMD describes EMDR as:

'a fairly new, non-traditional type of psychotherapy...growing in popularity, particularly for treating PTSD. It (EMDR) remains controversial among some health care professionals....It does not rely on talk therapy or medications. Instead, EMDR uses a patient's own rapid, rhythmic eye movements. These eye movements dampen the power of emotionally charged memories of past traumatic events...A treatment session can last up to 90 minutes. Your therapist will move his or her fingers back and forth in front of your face and ask you to follow these hand motions with your eyes. At the same time, the EMDR therapist will have you recall a disturbing event. This will include the emotions and body sensations that go along with it. Gradually, the therapist will guide you to shift your thoughts to more pleasant ones. Some therapists use alternatives to finger movements, such as hand or toe tapping or musical tones.'[19]

There are several other therapies available, some of them new, some of them which report good results when dealing with PTSD.

Not everyone has easy access to this kind of treatment. Regular, private treatment is expensive. There are some counsellors who work on a sliding fee scale to help make counselling possible for people in different financial circumstances. If you have insurance, you can check with your insurer to see what is included and how many sessions would be available.

If at all possible, get the help you need. If you are part of a church, ask around to see if there is an expert in the church who could help, or get someone to ask for professional recommendations for you. Look into options for health care where you can be referred to mental health professionals and counsellors, and receive cheaper or free treatment or medication for any associated problems such as depression. In the U.S., some places have free clinics for those on low income and without insurance. They sometimes have mental health professionals working in the clinic on a part-time basis. In the UK, the National Health Service (NHS) can help with various mental health services, but waiting times vary from area to area and there may be a long waiting list. It is a good idea to get on the list as soon as possible for an assessment. There are sometimes Emotional Coping Skills groups which teach skills for managing traumatic situations and symptoms. In the UK, you can also join health organisations such as Benenden[20] at a very low monthly cost which can provide six free counselling sessions after you have been a part of their health plan for six months. Six sessions is not much when ongoing treatment and care is needed, but it can at least get you started if your options are limited or the waiting list is long. If there is no counsellor nearby, sessions will be over the telephone. Even just six telephone sessions can make a difference in getting you through a particularly bad patch and helping you feel supported. If you are able to sacrifice financially and get the treatment you need for your health and recovery, then do so. Your health is worth it and your life is worth it.

Medications

Medication is often in the form of Selective Serotonin Reuptake Inhibitors (SSRIs) which regulate serotonin in the brain to help you feel better, or Serotonin-Norepinephrine Reuptake Inhibitors (SNRIs).[21] There are many different ones which help treat anxiety, depression or both. Many people find them helpful. However, it must be noted that they work for some and do not work for others. Side effects in the initial few weeks and even months of taking can, in some cases, be debilitating. Some people press on through this period and see positive results. Some people try several different types of SSRIs until they find one that works. For some, however, the negative side effects can be very serious (e.g. heightened depression, aggression, and suicidal feelings).[22]

Anti-depressants are not necessarily a quick route to feeling better. In my case, after four months trying two different medications, I could not function because of the severity of the side-effects and came off the medication gradually. I felt better off it than on it. Taking anti-depressants is a personal decision and the effects are different for different people so it is important not to create expectations in people. They will not know how it works for them personally until they have tried it.

As you take steps to look after yourself, don't be afraid to see a doctor, counsellor and appropriate mental health professional, or to use an anti-depressant under the supervision of a health professional. Medication is helpful for some people, and there is nothing to be ashamed of in getting all the help you can.

On balance, we need to recognise that these medications can also become addictive to the point where people are frightened to come off them. On a radio show I listened to with my husband, they talked with several people who had become addicted to the medications they were taking and there was no aftercare system in place to help them come off. While a good doctor should provide monitoring and a plan to help you come off the medication carefully, this does not always happen. If you do decide to go ahead with medication for trauma-related depression and anxiety, please take this into account and work out with a health professional a plan for how you can come off the medication over a period of time with appropriate help and support. I have also included a resource (UK) for beating addiction in the back of the book should the support of your local health care provider be insufficient. If you are not in the UK, you may be able to find something similar in your locality.

Aside from the conventional approach, there are also many things *you* can do yourself to help towards healing from the trauma you have experienced and all its consequences. They won't make everything better. They won't take it all away. But they will help significantly on your day to day journey.

There are also natural alternatives which are gaining recognition, being researched and used with some success although these are not yet used in mainstream health care. I will talk about these in this chapter under 'Natural Supplements & Alternative Remedies'.

Self-Care

Trauma, grief, PTS, PTSD & C-PTSD can also be helped through self-care and various self-help therapies. Get help as well if at all possible and as early as you can. Remember, if the symptoms caused by the trauma have been going on for a long time, at least one to three months, you should see a health professional such as a psychotherapist who may be able to diagnose PTSD or C-PTSD and take you through a programme of treatment. Do whatever you can to get help so that you do not have to bear this alone.

When professional help is necessary, we must remember however, that even with access to that treatment, we live most of our days in-between therapy appointments. A therapist can help us during sessions to know how to better cope with our thoughts and feelings during the week. They can enlighten us to negative thought habits and give us alternative approaches. However, there is also a lot that a therapist cannot do for us on an every-day basis.

What we do on all those normal days when we are alone, when we are not having a therapy session (if you are able to have them) is vitally important to our own survival and healing journey. That is where self-care comes in.

Self-care is just what it says it is. It is caring for yourself. When people are traumatised, they can lose motivation and energy to care for themselves in the same way as before. This can happen especially when there is depression as a result of the trauma. Self-care, however, is more important at this time than ever. This is the time for *you*. You need to nurture yourself.

If you had a broken leg, you would be forced to nurture yourself. You would need to have the medical help necessary. You would need to keep the leg raised, have someone help you get around in a wheelchair, and later learn to get around on crutches. You would need to eat nutritious food to ensure the healing of the bone. You would need to rest and find things to do that keep you busy and feeling engaged with things you enjoy in life. You would need to have physiotherapy and do exercises at home to regain strength and full mobility. To heal a broken leg, you would have no choice but to do these things if you want it to heal properly. I know because I had to go through three surgeries to heal a broken femur, the biggest bone in the body, after a horse riding accident.

It is marvellous that when a bone breaks and you take the necessary steps for it to heal, the bone begins to grow back. But before the bone grows back *inside* the break, it first begins to grow outside and around the break. It forms a bone callous around the break area to hold it strong while it fuses and heals inside. Ultimately, the extra bone that grows to repair a broken leg makes the bone in that leg stronger than in the leg that didn't break. We can take that as an encouragement in our healing journey that the broken areas in our souls can heal with more strength than before.

Just as you would have to care for and nurture a broken bone, self-care and nurture is vital in healing your brain. Because we can't see it the brain gets ignored. However, the brain is the hub of your life. It is the hub of your thoughts, creativity, movement, speech, senses, and personality. Neural pathways in the brain have been damaged and changed by the trauma you have experienced, but with care, your brain can heal. It may not heal exactly the same as it was before. The pathways may heal a bit differently to how they were before, but that's not a negative thing, they can change from the negative pathways that have been created through trauma into positive new pathways.

For this to happen, you need to put positive thoughts in your mind about yourself and your life. You also need good, positive, enjoyable experiences in your life to help bring healing to your brain. This is a process of baby steps. On some days it will feel like steps backwards. It is a process. The waves of pain and grief will still come, but you will find ways to ride them and survive, and they will gradually come less often, and gradually get smaller. You will have better days. You will have really bad days. On the bad days, show yourself grace and kindness. Your brain needs healing. It's a physiological issue. As well as engaging in prayer (for those who are of faith or would like to find faith), a physiological issue needs practical help.

The Practical Steps

Let's embark on the practical steps. But before you begin reading about the steps you can take to help yourself, I want to empathise once again with the pain and suffering you have experienced. Whether you were in the wrong place at the wrong time, suffered unexpected loss, a terrifying situation, or were calculatedly betrayed, mistreated, abused or abandoned, you have experienced a situation that is incredibly hard to bear and that we would not wish on another human being. Once again, I am sorry this happened with all my heart. It may not look like it right now, but there *is* a way forward.

The following are very practical and vital areas of self-care you can put into place in your own life to help you survive day by day, and embark on a journey towards healing. You probably won't be able to do all the steps at once. They are helpful steps you can begin to incorporate bit by bit as you are able. You can apply them in any order, and choose some of the suggestions that work for you. The first two steps, however, are not suggestions. These are essential for improved mental health and well-being. Let's begin with...

1. Good Nutrition

This is as practical as you can get. The food you put into your body becomes who you are. It feeds every cell including your brain cells. Junk food going in becomes junk coming out in the form of sickness and disease, lessened mental capacity, aging, forgetfulness, cancers,[23] Alzheimer's disease,[24] lowered immune system and an endless list of health issues. When you live on junk, your brain and body are not able to function at their full capacity. When you want to heal from trauma, you need your brain functioning the best it can, and you need to help it do that with good nutrition.

Maybe because of the trauma and its effects you don't want to eat well. Maybe you just feel like slobbing on a sofa with chips and a coke every day. Or maybe you don't feel like eating at all. Both of these positions are potentially harmful and even dangerous. You matter. You must care for yourself by eating well so that your body has the strength and nutrients it needs for recovery.

Alcohol, narcotics and nicotine are toxic to the body and brain. They are a form of poison. When traumatised, some people use or abuse substances to help numb the pain. However, long-term they will only cause damage, the pain of trauma will continue longer, and you will end up with even more problems in the form of ill health added to what you are already dealing with. They will prolong the pain and make recovery more difficult. They are self-defeating. You are worth more than that. If you use substances to help deal with trauma, please get help from local organisations, a counsellor and/or your church.

Food is the substance of our life, growth, and health on this earth. A spiritual life is vitally important too but to live on this earth you must eat! What you eat feeds your bloodstream and every cell in your body, including your brain. The health of your brain helps determine your responses to life, and your ability to deal with life and trauma. Toxic substances and junk foods will leave you poisoned and malnourished.

One lady I knew let her healthy diet slip after the loss of her husband because she was depressed and couldn't be bothered. But it only made her feel worse.

You need nutritious food, not junk food. Refined and sugary foods loaded with fats, salt, artificial colours, flavourings and preservatives, and sugary or artificially sweetened drinks stress the body. You don't need any more stress. Many people are in such a habit of eating junk food that it has become almost a cultural joke. In the U.S., the all-American meal is a hamburger, fries and a shake or Coke. The Western obsession and addiction to fast food, meat, and sodas has left many people with obesity, heart-related problems and other disease. For those who can afford it, a stent for the heart has become an almost 'normal' procedure. Some people cannot afford that kind of health care and yet continue to eat the junk food diet. Even worse however, is the fact that some people believe they have to eat junk food because they can't afford healthy food. In fact, one £5.00 or $6.99 McDonald's meal could buy the ingredients for a nutritious bean and vegetable stew for a family, or for two people as a dinner for a couple of days. That would be far more beneficial.

This book is not the place to get into the horrors of the modern, junk food diet and its consequences. It is the place however, to appeal to good sense, especially for those who are suffering trauma and PTSD and its off-shoot issues such as depression. It's also important for those who are caring for people in trauma. Good nutrition is vital! Just as you cannot expect the body to heal and recover so well from a disease if you feed it a junk food diet, you cannot expect that of the brain either. Give yourself every possible opportunity to recover by eating a healthy, whole food diet.

Cultural Differences

I'm always aware of and sensitive to this because I have lived in several countries. Different cultures eat different things, of course, so you would need to work out healthy eating within what your own culture has available. We have a huge cultural attachment to some foods, but this does not mean they are good for us. Be adventurous or go outside some of those norms if your culture's diet is not as healthy as it could be. For example, the Native Americans love fry bread but there is little nutrition in it and plenty of saturated fat and carcinogens from the cooking process. My family and I lived in China for several years, and the Chinese diet is healthy in many ways in that they eat a lot of vegetables and rice. However, some of them also eat a lot of pork which is not healthy. They also use copious amounts of salt, oil, salty sauces and monosodium glutamate (MSG), and much of the food is fried. The rice they eat is usually white. They also eat a lot of white flour products such as fried or steamed dumplings, delicious but in reality almost a Chinese equivalent of Western junk food. For a healthier diet, they could choose to eat more of the culture's nutritious stews and soups instead of so much fried food, change pork for poultry, eat more bean dishes in place of meat, eat brown rice instead of white, and cut back on the salt.

Your own culture will have healthier foods available so be sure to make the healthier choices for the sake of your mental, emotional and physical health.

In the West, we have no excuse for poor diet. Along with the mass availability of junk food is the huge availability of nutritious whole foods.

Often people eat things that are bad for them out of ignorance, or they still choose to eat them simply because it is a cultural habit and they have grown used to them and like the taste. However, all taste is acquired. Just as you can acquire a taste for what is essentially bad for you, you can change the habit of a lifetime for your taste buds and acquire a taste for what is good for you. You get a brand new set of taste buds approximately every two weeks that makes training them to appreciate whole foods much easier.[25]

Simple Steps to Healthier Eating

However you work it within your culture, these are some general rules that will help your body, your hormones, every system in your body, and your mood, be better balanced at a time when you really need it to be. Get someone who cares about you to help you with this if you need some outward motivation and encouragement. Here are some simple steps to healthier eating:

- Look at the ingredients! Don't just throw foods into your shopping trolley/cart in blind abandon and habit. Educate yourself as to what is inside that food.

- Avoid refined sugar products, especially sodas, candies and tinned foods laden with sugar and syrup. Do not eat high fructose corn syrup! Refined sugars stress the body and dampen the immune system. If you want a sweetener, try maple syrup, raw honey, or sweeten with dates and raisins, banana, apple or other fruit.

- Avoid refined white flour products such as white breads, white flour cookies and cakes, white rice and white pasta. Instead, eat wholegrain breads, wholegrain rice and pastas made with wholegrain flours and vegetables. This will increase vitamins and minerals, provide more fibre, improve digestion, be kinder to your colon, help avoid constipation, and feed your blood and brain better.

- Eat less meat. Meat is expensive. These days the animals are often subjected to horrendous feeding and other practices, given inappropriate, chemical-laden food, and slaughtered in stressful conditions. You get served up any chemicals the animal has eaten, and entrails, hairs and other remains in your sausages and hamburgers. If you are going to eat meat, avoid pork and processed meats high in nitrates, salts, and other substances your body won't thank you for, eat less red meat and more poultry. Also, eat meat from animals that are well cared for, pasture-raised, free from chemicals, and fed healthy, appropriate foods. What they eat goes into your body! Artificial fertilizers, pesticides, antibiotics and other chemicals will not help you heal but make you sick. In all honesty, you can find plenty of alternative sources of protein in things like beans such as chick peas (garbanzo), black, chilli, kidney, pinto and many others, and in green, red and brown lentils, quinoa, nuts, tofu, eggs (if you eat them), spinach, broccoli, soy milk, peas, seeds and peanut butter. A plant–based diet is becoming increasingly recommended and followed by many different types of people including top athletes. It is easier to digest, easier on the body, provides the necessary vitamins and minerals, boosts the immune system, and will provide you with more space and energy to heal.

- Eat less fried food, especially avoid deep fried and foods fried in cheap oils. If you cook with oil use coconut oil, or 'fry' in water. Eat more raw, fresh foods, vegetables, fruits, salads, lightly cooked/steamed vegetables, and food baked or grilled, or in soups or stews.

- Eat lots of fruit and vegetables. Eat lots of different colours. Eat plenty of dark green, leafy vegetables, and a variety of different coloured fruits. They are loaded with nutrition. Eat vegetables raw and/or lightly cooked. Eat ten portions a day or aim to be as close as possible. Iceberg lettuce is not included, neither are potato chips, fries, or the tomatoes in tomato ketchup! Eat proper, whole, fresh fruits and vegetables, not junk. Sprouted foods such as seeds like broccoli, radish and sprouted legumes like beans, chick peas and alfalfa are easy to grow in your own home all year round and bursting with anti-oxidants, vitamins and nutrients which will all help improve health and relieve stress in mind and body.

- Instead of drinking sodas, drink water, natural fruit juices with no added sugar which can be diluted a little with water (better for the teeth), fruit and herb teas including those native to your culture, and nut milks. The coffee culture might be nice for those used to it with all its tastes, trappings and caffeine-highs, but coffee is also responsible for some leaching of calcium from the bones, and the caffeine can cause insomnia and restlessness, caffeine-related headaches, exacerbate ulcers, and raise your blood pressure, cholesterol levels and heart rate. Remember, self-care is about caring for yourself and doing what will help you and your brain recover from trauma. Drink less coffee, don't drink it at bedtime or use it as a substitute for nutritious food or a replacement breakfast. Ensure you drink plenty of water to flush toxins out of the body and help your brain function well. If you use coffee as an energy boost to help you through trauma-associated lethargy, try using rhodiola rosea instead or ashwagandha. Both are natural supplements that can give your energy a boost without side-effects.

- Use natural supplements & alternative remedies. If you are able to afford multi-vitamins and minerals, buy food-source ones. Cheap vitamins and minerals get passed out of the body without the goodness being absorbed, achieving nothing and wasting your money. A good quality multi-vitamin and mineral is helpful. For women, a B-complex supplement is vital help for balancing mood. Vitamin C can help boost your immune system. To aid sleep at bedtime, calcium helps. Calcium contains tryptophan, a natural sleep aid. Magnesium is often deficient in our Western lifestyles leaving us stressed, so a magnesium supplement is helpful for relaxation and can be bought in a formulation balanced with calcium and vitamin D3.

The most important thing is to have a healthy, nutritious diet. However, because of over-farming, poor soils and lack of variety, we need supplements to help with deficiencies, especially at a time when the body and mind are traumatised, using a lot of extra energy, and need good nutrition. Supplements can also help give the confidence that you are getting all necessary minerals.

There are also natural supplements you can take to help with trauma-associated depression such as rhodiola rosea, selenium and SAM-e. Rhodiola should contain 3% rosavin for best effect. There is increasing evidence that circumin in turmeric, in the concentrated form called BCM-95 is very helpful in relief from depression at a dose of 1000mg per day. Results from this are proving so good in some circles that it is being considered as a more widely used possible future alternative for depression treatment. It is also anti-inflammatory which will aid the body in stress recovery.

- Eat breakfast. This really is the most important meal of the day. Not only does it give energy to start a new day, but eating a healthy and nutritious breakfast on a regular basis is linked to many health benefits, including improved concentration and performing better at work, a healthy body-weight, and control over blood sugar levels (important in preventing or controlling diabetes).

  When you eat, you want to feed your brain with plenty of nutrients. A healthy breakfast meal should contain a variety of foods, including fruits or vegetables, whole grains, low- or non-fat dairy, and lean protein. Good options include: oat porridge and muesli, wholegrain cereals (not high sugar), with some wholegrain toast and natural peanut butter, sliced banana, omelette and boiled egg, and smoothies and juices made of green veggies and fruit with flaxseed.

There are so many colourful, nutrition-laden, filling recipes available these days which are also quick to make. Coffee, doughnuts, or sugary packet cereals just won't feed your brain with what you need to give yourself the best chances of feeling better. You are worth more than that.

Eating is one of life's pleasures that you can enjoy. Don't use it as a 'drug' to ease pain, as that can lead to obesity and poor health, and just make you feel worse about yourself at a time when you need to feel good. But eating in a balanced and whole way can be a medicine for the body. This quote, attributed to Hippocrates in approximately 400BC says much about how a healthy way of eating can help your body, including your brain. 'Let food be thy medicine, and medicine be thy food.'

I know it can be easy to not care and to slip into bad habits at a time of trauma and depression, overeating, undereating, and using junk food as a comfort food. However, it won't help you. Good nutrition is your first step to managing better and feeling better.

2. Exercise & Sleep

Exercise increases blood flow to the brain. This helps reduce stress and anxiety, calms, relaxes, and makes you feel better and more confident. Even chewing your food is an exercise that increases blood flow to the brain. Get out and get sunshine. You need sunshine for Vitamin D which is significant in recovery from depression. Don't sit in front of the television all the time, or spend hours scrolling down Facebook or on other social media sites or video games. None of these will aid towards recovery, and too much time on sites like Facebook is now known to contribute to depression. Comparison is inevitable and Facebook makes everyone else look happy and okay when you are not. It is a lie of course but social media is known for making others' lives look great through smiley photos and gloss! Instead of living in a virtual reality, get out and about and get the body moving while you inhale fresh air. Get out and meet real people face-to-face. Even a short time doing that will be more beneficial to health than a 'virtual' life on social media.

A few simple stretching exercises each day can help you feel so much better about life and yourself. Try jogging up the stairs, around your yard/garden/neighbourhood, or running in pleasant surroundings with as clean air as possible. Listen to music as you exercise. If jogging or running doesn't appeal or is hard on your knees, try power-walking. Power-walking works the muscles including the heart with less strain on joints than running, and gives you more opportunity to enjoy what's around you.

During prolonged periods of stress caused by trauma and grief, adrenal gland function can be affected. This is known as adrenal fatigue and can cause symptoms such as tiredness, weakness and depression, nausea, loss of appetite and salt cravings. If this occurs, exercise is still beneficial but do something gentler like power-walking instead of running or working out in the gym, or do gentle stretching and strengthening workouts. This can provide stress relief from PTSD, detox the body, and bring healing without taxing the adrenal glands.

Join a group where you can exercise together such as a yoga class, cycling, swimming, or hiking, play a sport, and enjoy encouraging company as well as healthful movement.

Deep breathing is a very useful exercise for increasing oxygen levels, relieving anxiety and stress, relaxing tensed muscles, and helps to make you feel more centred and grounded. Try the following:

- Sit or stand
- Take a deep breath in through the nose to the count of five. Your diaphragm, just at the bottom of the rib cage, should push out as you inhale air and your shoulders should not go up
- Hold that breath for two seconds
- Breathe out through the mouth slowly to the count of five
- Relax and repeat
- As you do this, you can shut your eyes, relax your muscles, and feel the benefits
- Now, lift both shoulders towards your ears. Push your shoulders back and let them gently drop. Bring them back to their normal position. Do this rotation slowly five times, breathing slowly.

I got a gathering of Native American people doing this breathing exercise once when speaking on trauma at a large tent meeting in the desert. An 'aah' of stress relief and relaxation went across everyone there.

Some muscles in the body have a tendency to hold trauma in them. They can be tense throughout the day without you even realising. This can happen especially in the shoulders, neck, jaw, and back, and in the legs too.

My daughter is an excellent, award-winning massage therapist. I went to her for a massage one day for some relief from long-term pain in the buttock and back which I had attributed to either sciatica or piriformis syndrome. She informed me that the iliopsoas, a big set of muscles running from the back through the pelvis and thighs, can hold stressful memories. Understanding how and where my body was holding tension, having a massage, and doing exercises to stretch that muscle freed me from years of constant pain. Knowledge really can bring greater freedom. Just understanding the root of something can be a vital part of healing. If you can afford it, or have a kind friend or patient spouse, massage can be therapeutic, creating a sense of well-being and relieving stress. There is much to be said for the power of touch.

Dancing is a wonderful form of exercise which you can do with a dance video or make up your own. Using music that brings healing, happiness, energy or all of these, movement to music is powerfully healing for the body and soul.

Dancing releases endorphins which promote a feeling of well-being. You can dance alone just for the sheer fun of it, dance with someone else, or join a dance class. Before C-PTSD, I could be very consistent about exercising. After having C-PTSD and being post-menopausal at the same time, it was as if all willpower and motivation flew out the window. I didn't get out as much, had little desire to drive anywhere, and going to a gym was not possible financially. For the best part of two years of C-PTSD, I had no motivation to exercise. After seeing the doctor, I received 16 free gym visits on the UK National

Health Service (a wonderful service). I kept that up for almost the entire 16 visits but due to illness could not complete all of them. Then we moved away from that area. No exercise just increased the bad feelings about myself caused by the trauma. I knew I had to do something to help myself in the form of exercise. To motivate and keep myself interested, I set up three kinds of physical exercise so that I could do something according to my mood and ability. Some days, I do 10-20 minutes on an exercise bike. Some days, I power walk up the hill near where we live and back again. And on other days I put high energy music on and just dance. I learnt a lot of aerobic and stretch moves over the years so it is fun to incorporate those into a dance routine with a whole lot of moves just made up on the spot too.

On days when you just can't find the energy, some good music helps and it is better to do even a little than none at all. Having a choice of simple forms of exercise means there is always something I can do which doesn't require a lot of effort in getting somewhere. I don't need anything that puts me off. I don't need to set myself up for failure and neither do you. Set up some kind of exercise in your life that works for you at least most of the time.

To survive trauma, I believe exercise is essential. It releases essential feel-good chemicals that have been deprived from your body for too long because of the trauma. It increases your energy and makes you feel better, improving your confidence and motivation.

Exercising to music or exercising outdoors in fresh air and nature are like a double dose of medication, physical and soul therapy all at the same time. If you have a beach near you, walk on it, walk the dog, go for hikes in beautiful places, get on a bike and just cycle away stress. Find a way to enjoy engaging your body in activity and movement.

Sufficient Sleep

I can't emphasise enough the importance of getting plenty of sleep! Sleep is healing. Healing and repair take place while you are sleeping and that includes in the brain. Trauma can interrupt sleep with dreams, nightmares, flashbacks, anxiety, and the inability to relax, and tiredness can just make everything feel worse. But you can help yourself and reduce the chances of this with some simple steps:

- Don't drink so much coffee. Don't drink caffeinated drinks. This is especially important the later it gets in the day. Drink sleep-promoting herbal teas instead such as lemon balm and chamomile which help you relax.

- Try not to eat late and go to bed on a full stomach. If your body is busy digesting food it will find it harder to rest well.

- Listen to gentle, quiet music, nothing depressing and not too inspirational as this will energise you at the wrong time of day. You can use the videos I mentioned earlier with calming words and healing music, and have them playing quietly with the screen down so you are not watching it.

- Don't look at computer screens last thing at night. Make sure you finish with computers well before bedtime. It is a fact that blue screen use (phone, computer or tablet) too close to bedtime interferes with sleep.[26]

- Don't start thinking about traumatic events at bedtime. I know this is easier said than done as flashbacks and thoughts come involuntarily. We are often less distracted as we go to bed and prepare for sleep and that is when the mind can start thinking about negative events. However, if you are listening to helpful and soothing words and music instead, this will distract the mind and fill it with something else.

- Ensure you are getting enough calcium and magnesium, both of which aid stress relief and relaxation.

- Eat tryptophan-containing foods to aid sleep such as raw almonds, turkey, chicken, and whole grains but only small amounts close to bedtime, just a small snack. A cup of hot milk with a little honey can also be helpful.[27]

You will probably need more sleep than usual. This is perfectly alright. If work gets you up early or keeps you out late, find times when you can take an extra nap to make up for it. Just take naps anyway. Try not to go to bed late as it makes you tired and wears down the immune system. It is much harder to deal with the symptoms of trauma when you are tired and worn out.

Equally, it is important to make sure that you get up in the morning. Getting so much sleep that you don't get out of bed leaves you purposeless and listless. Develop healthy habits that make you feel good about yourself. Remember, it is not a performance. You are not trying to impress anybody. This is all about your needs. Sleeping is a time to let go. It is a time to be comfortable and relaxed. And if you need more sleep, enjoy it!

A bedtime routine helps. I have certain supplements I take at bedtime including calcium and magnesium. I make myself a calming herbal tea. I don't drink much of it, just a few small sips, but knowing it is there helps, and if I wake up in the night I can drink more of it. Even if the drink is cold it still helps. I use essential oils at night to help me relax too. I usually use lavender oil at bedtime, putting a few drops on my hand which I then pat around my neck and chest. Lavender oil is very relaxing. The smell of it also signals to my body and brain that it is time to sleep. Do things that make you feel good at bedtime, and that prepare you for sleep.

Of course, filling your mind with words of comfort and reassurance at bedtime is very effective. You may have certain poems or phrases you find helpful. I have often used the Bible as it is full of comforting words. There are scriptures that also refer specifically to sleep and night time.

> 'My whole being shall be satisfied as with marrow and fatness; and my mouth shall praise You with joyful lips when I remember You and meditate on You in the night watches. For You have been my help, and in the shadow of your wings will I rejoice. My whole being follows hard after you and clings closely to You: Your right hand upholds me.'[28]

> 'You give your beloved sleep.'[29]

> 'In the multitude of my anxious thoughts within me, Your comforts cheer and delight my soul.'[30]

When going through trauma and PTSD, I had a difficult time concentrating while reading a book. It was hard to take it in so well. Sometimes, I found a book that worked better, with shorter chapters, or easier reading and found I could take in more. One book that I found helpful was a book of prayer. This book, *The Edge of Glory*, is a book of prayers in the Celtic tradition. The repetitive, soothing nature of these short prayers makes them easy to pray out loud and focus on, and they leave beautiful images in the mind. They are simple requests addressing the basic needs in life and often based on thoughts around the beauty of nature and creation. Here are three examples. You might find these helpful for yourself.

Calm me O Lord as you stilled the storm
Still me O Lord, keep me from harm
Let all the tumult within me cease
Enfold me Lord in your peace.

God in the night
God at my right
God all the day
God with me stay
God in my heart
Never depart
God with thy might
Keep me in light
Through this dark night.

Deep peace of the running wave to you
Deep peace of the flowing air to you
Deep peace of the quiet earth to you
Deep peace of the shining stars to you
Deep peace of the Son of peace to you.[31]

As you slowly speak prayers like this, or poems and prose with healing words of your own choosing, you can see how the repetition and simplicity of them absorb into your soul bringing healing and peace. I found this book helpful because it had words specifically for bedtime, first thing in the morning, and other times of day. Repetitive, flowing words like this are easy to say and leave peaceful images and feelings in the heart and mind. This is a form of meditation. Whatever words you use and wherever you find them, a soothing poem, a word of comfort from a friend or loved one, words are powerful tools to help you feel more relaxed and ready to sleep.

3. Be Creative

Creativity is starting to take a front seat in therapy for trauma and PTSD. In trauma, creativity is often one of the first things that suffers, and yet, it is one of the most healing activities you can engage in.

Art

For example, just twenty minutes of art therapy reduces stress hormones, distracts the mind, uses a different part of the brain, relaxes and produces feel-good hormones, gives a sense of achievement, is rewarding, can help to improve confidence, and builds ability to focus again.[32]

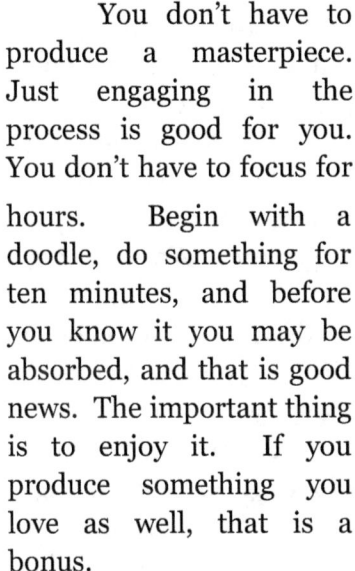

You don't have to produce a masterpiece. Just engaging in the process is good for you. You don't have to focus for hours. Begin with a doodle, do something for ten minutes, and before you know it you may be absorbed, and that is good news. The important thing is to enjoy it. If you produce something you love as well, that is a bonus.

Try a Zentangle. This one I did looks complicated, but it is surprisingly simple. All you need for this is a black pen and paper. Draw a square on paper, about 4" x 4". Make some lines from side to side, top to bottom, in one continuous movement if you like, or separate movements. These lines can curve and be wavy or straight. Now you have a square with shapes inside. Fill these shapes with patterns of your own choosing, from things you see around you or from your own imagination. You can make these Zentangles as simple or as complicated as you like. You can include words inside them that speak something important to you.

Using Your Hands

One man in the UK had been a soldier in the British army and suffered trauma and PTSD. He got psychiatric help but also took up pottery. He had never done pottery before but enjoyed it so much that he now has his own kiln for firing and sells his pottery online. He has found it extremely helpful for PTSD symptoms and recovery.[33]

You may have other creative skills such as jewellery making or painting, knitting, crochet, woodwork, etc. Perhaps you are musical and write songs. You can turn song-writing into an outlet for the trauma. Work out your anxiety and stress through playing an instrument, or creating something with your hands rather than allowing the trauma to steal your creativity. If you don't consider yourself a very creative person, you may discover something new about yourself. Be creative in your own way. It might be cooking or gardening, or rearranging a room. It is all outworking creativity. Where trauma has tried to steal from you and your life, let your life be filled with creative and constructive productivity instead.

Music

Music is a wonderful therapy. Research shows that music therapy can improve self-esteem, decrease anxiety and depression, reduce muscle tension, increase motivation, release emotions, and improve relationships.[34] My oldest daughter has a friend trained in music therapy which she uses for early intervention with children who have a disability. Music can be healing.

Listen to music which helps. You will soon know what is helpful and what is not. If you listen to music that makes you feel sad or depressed, turn it off. If it makes you feel heavy and angry or dark, you don't need that. Listen to music that soothes your soul or provides positive energy. You can find beautiful 'morning' music to get you started positively in the morning, and relaxing music to engage your mind and prepare you for restful sleep. I sometimes listen to light, happy music in the morning and atmospheric music with the sound of waves and sea gulls in the evening. You can find music online that is written in certain tones (binaural beats) which is said to help the brain.[35] If you can't get online or don't have suitable technology, see if someone can get you a music CD to play. Or turn on a radio and listen to something you love.

Sometimes, singing and worship can become hard when experiencing trauma. I am a trained singer and I write songs, but when I suffered trauma, I stopped doing it like I was before. It gradually returned, however, and I found I could write in a new way. As I said, creativity can suffer, but it can also find a new beauty. Beautiful music and beautiful sights and sounds are more important in your life now than ever. If you can't sing or play an instrument you can listen to something that creates positive emotions and engages the brain. It is important not to allow your thoughts to freewheel, involuntarily revolving the traumatic situations around and around in your mind. Music is very helpful for preventing this, filling the mind, helping you survive, and bringing healing to the brain and body.

Writing

Writing is another creative way to have an outlet for your feelings. You can use writing to record what works for you and when it works as you deal with trauma. You can speak to yourself through your writing, make your complaints, and write prayers and poems. You can illustrate a journal too with pen or pencil drawings, or magazine pictures and text. Writing your experiences into a poem or stories can be a helpful way to get feelings out and even share them with others.

I lost much creativity after experiencing trauma, and books I had almost finished writing were put on hold for over three years or more. This book went on hold for a long time. But when I was able I did find help in writing some simple poems for my grandchildren, and a few songs I wrote contained a beauty that had not been there before. When I started writing again sporadically over that time, my writing was more honest and less afraid of what others might think. I was more able to address issues head on, and convey greater compassion. You may find you have much to say that comes out more easily in writing. You may even want to communicate with others and encourage them in their journey as you survive and journey yourself.

Gardening & Nature

Gardening is an extremely helpful form of therapy. Therapeutic Horticulture and Horticultural Therapy are names being given to the use of the healing power of gardening and plant-based activities, to help people suffering from mental illness, PTSD, and various disabilities.

Getting outside in the fresh air and nurturing a garden is incredibly good for you. The Creator of the first garden knew that when He created man and put him in a beautiful garden. The relationship between nature and man is simple but powerfully healing. When you grow plants, tend them, water them, pull weeds, watch them bud and flower, and maybe eat your own home-grown fruits and vegetables, you get a 'sense of well-being from treating something well.'[36] While some doctors are slow to recognise natural forms of treatment, others are actively promoting this activity which is 'as old as the hills' as an effective treatment. It is hoped that 'horticultural therapy will soon become as normal as cognitive behavioural therapy.'[37] This would be good news for people for whom some medications and treatments are not working or are too expensive.

'Doctors have not yet accepted that something so simple can be more effective than drugs. But we know it works. In contact with nature, our brains are triggered into a reduced-stress mode.'

'The green gym is particularly beneficial for people with mental ill health, depression, anxiety and dementia.'[38]

My father was a wonderful gardener and an arborist (tree expert). He turned to his garden in times of stress and found great solace and comfort there.

There have been too many moves and transitions in my life to establish a garden until more recently. However, when I did have the opportunity to create a garden it was thrilling to discover how much I enjoyed it, and how much it ministered to my soul and helped my mind. The fresh air, exercise, the enjoyable work of nurturing plants, eating what you have grown, and the growing relationship between the plants and yourself, is for me better than taking a medication. The plants became my 'plant babies' and nurturing them got my mind off myself. Now, I would not be without a space for growing things.

Start Small. The idea of planning and preparing an entire garden might seem beyond your capacity or creativity at the moment. Perhaps you feel overwhelmed at the thought, especially if you have never really grown anything before. However, big things can grow from a small 'seed'. You could begin with preparing just a small area outside by digging the soil, adding some compost, and planting something simple and happy like sunflowers, or growing some climbing beans to eat. You could plant a seed in a pot of compost and watch it grow. You might find that your very small beginning turns into something so enjoyable that you want to do more. I found expending energy on lugging heavy paving stones, raking gravel, and digging hard earth very stress relieving. For some time, however, I was very low and had no energy for the heavier jobs. Instead, I planted a few seeds and deadheaded flowers. These little jobs are therapeutic too.

Artists and interior designers have long believed that colour can dramatically affect moods, feelings, and emotions. While psychologists dispute the scientific evidence for colour psychology, green is a colour that symbolizes nature and the natural world. Green is often used in decorating for its calming effect (for example, in waiting rooms or hospital birthing rooms), and is thought to relieve stress and promote healing. The colour blue calls to mind feelings of calmness or serenity. It is often described as a peaceful or tranquil colour.[39] Both of these colours can be experienced when we are out in the garden and in nature.

Gardening really does help to change the way the brain works and brings healing to it. In the UK there are opportunities to spend time with gardening groups specially set up for therapeutic and social purposes.[40] You or a friend or relative could look up what opportunities there might be in your country and area. Even getting along once a week to participate in a gardening programme with others would be beneficial. Or it could be arranged for you to join a friend who has a garden.

However you are able to do it and however small you can begin, it is a highly beneficial activity for people suffering from trauma and PTSD because of its healing effect on the brain, the social possibilities, and the chance to learn new skills. Some people have even gone on to do further training and find jobs in horticulture which has given them a new lease of life.

Getting Out in Nature. Of course, you don't have to do gardening to receive the therapeutic benefits of plants, although tending plants has a benefit of caring for and nurturing something, and reaping the rewards and satisfaction of its growth. You can receive huge benefits just from being outside in nature.[41] In fact, at any time it is essential to your well-being, but especially when managing trauma.

The fresh air, the stimulus of natural textures, colours, smells and sights is relaxing, calming and inspiring for the senses and promotes positive feelings of well-being. Feeling the crunch of stones and sticks beneath your feet, or the soft tread of the earth, the softness of grass, the brush of leaves against your skin, the touch of the sun's rays on your face (including getting your daily dose of vitamin D), are all highly beneficial sensations.

The wind blowing your hair can literally feel like it is blowing away the cares, troubles and 'cobwebs'. Enjoying the salty air of the seacoast is particularly refreshing and healing. Woodlands and forests, vast expanses of heathery moorland, rolling hills and rocky dales, and rivers and streams flowing through lush countryside can bring a sense of tranquility and serenity. Hearing the sounds of nature, the scuffles of a retreating vole or mouse in a hedgerow, bird song, the 'knocking' of a woodpecker, the breeze through the leaves or water over rocks is all therapy for the heart, mind and body.

Try to get outside and enjoy nature as much as possible. The beauty of the natural world is a wonderful gift which brings healing to the human soul.

Trauma can steal the sense, awareness and enjoyment of beauty. I know that from my own experience, but that enjoyment can also return. Each time you get outside and allow yourself to be embraced by the natural world it can help, and gradually that awareness, enjoyment, and even wonder, can be restored.

4. Handling Troublesome Images & Negativity

It is normal to process issues. It is the brain's way of answering questions, finding a 'safe place' in your mind to put events, helping you come to a place of acceptance, resolution, a way of thinking, or knowing what to do. When trauma happens, however, normal processing can be disturbed. In PTSD, troublesome and disabling images come back to your mind on a daily basis, often many times day and night. It is therefore helpful to have self-care methods for dealing with such images and flashbacks when they enter your mind and seek to derail you.

There are many 'mindfulness' techniques that you can use to help. These bring you back 'into the moment', taking your mind off the past and bringing you into the present. They can involve looking at an object in the distance, focussing on it, and using breathing techniques while you relax and bring your body and mind into a more peaceful state. Different counsellors use variations of these techniques as well as more well-known treatments such as Cognitive Behavioural Therapy or Eye Movement Desensitisation and Reprocessing (EMDR). Mindfulness is becoming increasingly popular and there are many approaches. You may hear words like *centring, grounding, tapping,* and *meditation.*

Useful Tools:

People are all different, their traumatic experience is different, the way they respond to it is different. Therefore they will find different techniques help them personally. People can adopt personalised 'tools' that help them to deal with such invasive images. You can choose whatever tool you wish that is helpful to you. Here are some examples:

Tool #1 – Visualisation

In my case, I chose to visualise the image of a scrubbing brush. The traumatic images had become ingrained in my mind over a period of three years. To defend myself from their invasive nature I needed something that would reach into the 'grain' of the material of my mind and scrub out the images. For some reason, I chose a wooden scrubbing brush. I like wooden-handled tools and equipment so perhaps that is why. The brush I visualise has a groove on each side so it is easy to hold. The bristles are of natural material and very stiff and strong. The traumatic images have no choice but to disappear as I use this brush of choice to scrub them away. As a believer in Christ who died to take my sin and rose again to give me life, the blood He shed for me is considered cleansing and counted very precious. So, I visualise using the blood of Jesus as a kind of 'cleaning fluid' that I use with my scrubbing brush. As I scrub the image with the blood of Jesus, the image begins to disappear from even the deepest, most ingrained places. Over a period of time, that image has become more and more erased and less powerful.

For someone else their tool could be a paintbrush which paints over the unwanted image. It might be a mop with a bucket of soapy water. It might be a simple eraser. You might imagine a computer delete function which wipes it off the screen of your mind. My daughter, who was also traumatised by the same event which affected me, said it felt like a box in the room of her mind. Wherever she went, there was the box in the way, waiting to be tripped over. It could be ignored some of the time but was always there. I could identify with the feeling. As she explained the trauma as a box that was always there, I imagined a sledge hammer. Again it was wooden, and it had a long wooden handle. I lifted the sledge hammer and with both hands brought it crashing down on that box. I did it again, and again, and the box began to break up. As it began to break up, it also began to lose its power in my thinking.

Whatever tool is helpful to you, remember it is not a destructive weapon. What I mean is that the tool you use is not used to do nasty things to people in your mind. Smashing a box is not the same as imagining smashing people. You are not scrubbing out as a kind of revenge with feelings of malice. That would not be good for you. Neither are you acting in a way that resembles an obsessive compulsive disorder (OCD). You are not scrubbing and scrubbing, unable to remove the images. That would not be good for you either. The key thing to remember is choosing a tool in your mind that works for you personally. As you use it in a measured way it brings about constructive and helpful results, removing the power of the images and releasing you into greater freedom.

Tool #2 - Replacement Words & Images (PTSD to PRST)

If you have suffered trauma, are experiencing symptoms of PTSD and have been diagnosed with PTSD or C-PTSD, suddenly it seems like you have taken on a new persona. Where has the old *you* gone? Where is the happy you? Life can feel surreal. Nothing seems normal like it did. The words Post Traumatic Stress Disorder become a big part of your life and vocabulary.

It is necessary to understand what PTSD is and to know if you are suffering with it, so that you can take the necessary steps to deal with it. However, after some time, it can feel like your whole life and self revolves around the words PTSD. It can become a label with which you refer to yourself and think about yourself. When that happens, it can become unhelpful. When we become defined or define ourselves by the words PTSD on a long-term basis, we can reinforce beliefs, mindsets, habits of thinking, negative thoughts, negative feelings, and feelings of being trapped in something out of which we cannot rise. It can be hard to do, but at some point, we must begin to develop a new image of ourselves that is more positive than 'post-traumatic stress disorder'.

The idea of having PTSD can become consuming. I knew that I was never going to get beyond it unless I found another way to see myself. I will share my own experience of this with you in the hope that you too can find replacement words and images for the label of 'PTSD' or 'traumatised'.

As a person of faith, a Christian, the Bible has always been very important to me. Its words and the God behind them have been my help, strength, support, guidance, comfort and encouragement for many years. When I suffered trauma, my faith took a tremendous hit. I struggled for a long time to be able to focus on the words of the Bible which before had been so encouraging. That made the trauma I had been through feel even worse. I felt like I had lost everything, my family, my work, my peace of mind, all I had worked to achieve, and my faith too. It was too much to bear. The loss of three years to PTSD wore me down to the point where life did not seem worth living and I felt suicidal.

One day, I tried to read for just a few seconds from the Bible which had always been such a help, but which now, in my misfortune, seemed so hard to read. I managed to read just a few lines from Isaiah chapter 54. There it says that the heritage (inheritance) of those who believe in the Lord is peace, righteousness, security, and triumph over opposition. I had read it often, in good and bad times, but for months now in extreme distress and trauma, it almost seemed to mock me. This time, however, something different happened. I noticed the first letter of each of those words.

Peace = P
Righteousness = R
Security = S
Triumph over opposition = T

PRST. I said it out loud. It sounded a bit like PTSD. But it wasn't. It wasn't Post-Traumatic Stress Disorder. It was something positive. It was peace, righteousness, security, and triumph over opposition. It was PRST instead of PTSD.

So each time PTSD, its name, its label, its images and symptoms interrupted me and my thoughts, I began to replace it with the words, 'No, I won't live by PTSD. I have PRST.' The effect on my mind and ability to cope was positive from the start. My perception of myself and my health and well-being improved, and the symptoms became easier to cope with. It wasn't an instant miracle, but it was as if in the recesses of my brain, where such a dark place had developed over time, a tiny flicker of light was switched on and the ability to hope again was gently re-ignited. It was going to be a process and need practice, but re-defining and replacing the words PTSD with something positive gave hope for my future. You could think of some replacement words and images for yourself for the letters P.T.S.D. You could do the same with the letters T.R.A.U.M.A. and G.R.I.E.F. too. The purpose is not to deny what you are dealing with but to shift the controlling and all-consuming nature of PTSD and trauma's effects, and give the mind new space for hope and healing.

Words and beliefs are very powerful. I truly believe that my brain responded to the change in perception through a simple change of words. I could feel the difference. It was a tentative start but I continued to do this, speaking out PRST each time thoughts of PTSD came to my mind and it has helped begin the reconstruction of new and positive pathways in my brain.

A few weeks after this discovery, I noticed an advertisement for an online course in PTSD recovery. The person had had a lot of success with the techniques they encouraged. It was too expensive for me to do the course but I sat through the introductory hour of explanation of the course. During that time I heard the repeated message that recovery from PTSD was possible. As I listened, I noticed another positive response in my brain. PTSD is notoriously difficult to treat and cure for many reasons. However, when that is the message we keep hearing from articles, health professionals and other sources, we can feel as if we have descended into a terrible, frightening and incurable place from which we can never escape. This is *not* helpful! However, the message I was hearing was that we *can* recover. Once we can start to believe that we can recover from trauma and PTSD, that it *is* possible, we have taken a step in a positive direction towards recovery. There will be work involved to replace the negative images, thoughts and words with positive ones, but it is a beginning. Knowing that brings hope. And where there is hope, survival and healing is possible.

Tool #3 - Positive Words & Self-Talk

I cannot stress enough the importance of positive words and self-talk. Everything about trauma and grief seems to pull you on a daily, even hourly basis, towards negativity of thoughts in the words you use and into a downward spiral. It can be extremely difficult, if not impossible at times, to think and speak positively when traumatised, but it is one of the major keys to survival.

Often, flashbacks to painful events, frightening thoughts, and waves of grief come rolling in when you are in the middle of doing some task, working round the house, writing an email, when you are tired in the evening, getting into bed, or waking up in the morning. Flashbacks can also cause panic in the night. It is a daily battle to keep fighting off thoughts and negative images. We need all the help we can get in developing positive words and self-talk.

Use Motivational Videos

A useful source of help, I have found, is motivational videos. You can listen to them online. There are hundreds of them. You can listen to a whole playlist and play them from the time you get up in the morning until you go to bed. If silence is helpful at times for restoration and recovery, that is good. However, when quietness becomes an opportunity for negative thoughts and images, motivational videos can fill that gap with positive thoughts that will do just what they say, motivate you. Many of them have accompanying videos. You don't need to watch all these. You can just turn the volume up and listen to the inspiring and motivating words while you get on with your day. Often the words are put to inspirational music too so you get the best of music and positive words at the same time.

I have found motivational videos really helpful for depression and feelings of hopelessness. Just type 'motivational videos' into your online search and a whole host of them will appear. I don't always agree with everything that is said on them. Choose wisely. You want to listen to what truly helps, the point being that they are positive and motivating! I can just move on to another one if I don't like one. There are some excellent and inspiring Christian motivational videos too. You might not want to listen to one that challenges you to pray more when you are struggling with praying at all! Videos about big achievements and success might not help right now, but if they do, then use them. Choose the ones that really encourage and help you to have a positive day.

You can upload videos to your computer and turn them on at the touch of a button or two first thing in the morning to help get your mind off to a positive start. In the evening, you can also find more chilled-out versions of motivational videos set to music. These help you to relax and unwind, and put good things into your mind. If you have the ability to do so, you can even have them playing all night so that if you wake up and can't sleep, you can listen to the soothing and healing words and music as you lie there. This will help to prevent your mind from wandering onto negative things in the night and help you get back to sleep, or at least into a mentally restful place.

If you have older technology and no computer or internet capacity to do the above, try asking someone to record things for you so that you can listen to them on a tape or CD. You may even be able to record some positive, encouraging words of your own, or read them from a book as you record them, so that you can listen back to them.

Creative & Comedy Television/Radio

Sometimes, you just want to kick back, unwind and not have to *do* anything! You just want to be distracted and not have to think at all. That is okay. People do this all the time by watching TV or listening to the radio. However, hours of television won't be helpful. This is a time of your life when you need to feel that you are productive in some way, that you are getting somewhere on your journey of healing, even if only in baby steps. So it is better to engage as much as you can in the other healing steps mentioned here than spend hours in front of the TV. However, for the times when it is helpful, comedies and stand-up comedians make wonderful entertainment and distraction, and the laughter is good for your health, releasing feel-good chemicals called endorphins which relieve pain.

I watched a British comedy panel show called, *'Would I Lie to You?'* The clever use of words appealed to my love for language, was very stimulating, and the ridiculous humour made me laugh so much. I didn't want to stop watching because it was just so good to laugh!

Something else I found helpful at times was a good old detective series. I don't like the crimes themselves, and murder is obviously not a happy subject but traumatic, so I didn't watch those bits. But I did enjoy the stimulation of seeing how a crime was solved. It engaged my mind and I enjoyed the way the characters cleverly solved the crime. However, I noticed that watching too many of these became unhelpful in the form of images and dark thoughts. Watching one occasionally was fine. Use the TV or other entertainment to feed the soul in a wholesome way through comedy, helpful movies and series, programmes that teach you a new skill or help you learn, that are informative or interesting, but not dark, depressing or engaging you in a lot of 'virtual reality' stress.

A word of caution: if you are a more sensitive person, and especially if you have a vivid imagination, putting those kinds of images in the mind may not be helpful. If you wake up with those images in your mind in the morning, don't watch those kinds of TV series. You don't want to give yourself more negative and unhelpful images and thoughts to deal with. You need all the positive images and thoughts you can put in. That applies to everyone suffering trauma, not just people who are sensitive. All people in trauma are sensitive in some way, so be careful what you watch and listen to, note results and don't do the things that are unhelpful. I found watching a good comedy was far more healing!

While TV and other forms of entertainment such as theatre performances can be helpful distractions from the bombardment of thoughts trauma can cause, try to watch things that are constructive, creative, and helpful towards healing. As well as the comedy mentioned, one of the helpful programmes I watched was a British show called, "Money for Nothing", where the show hosts collect unwanted old items from a dump and creatively turn them into treasures that they then sell. It was great to watch and I learned something at the same time.

Be careful of the material you watch. The emphasis needs to be on *wholesome* entertainment. If you use the television or internet or videos to watch pornographic material to make you feel better, you are on dangerous ground and a downhill slope. Watching sexual content does indeed release dopamine, a feel-good chemical, into the body. However, the need for this becomes addictive. That is why people who indulge in pornography often can't stop watching it and have to watch pornography that becomes increasingly graphic and in some cases, violent. This is not the sort of stimulation your mind needs for recovery. If you are struggling with this, don't be ashamed to ask for help from someone who can help you stop.

Speaking Positively

In trauma the brain is grappling, trying to sort through what has happened and find an answer, a place to sit, to rest. As mentioned in Chapter 2, the normal pathways in the brain may not be functioning in the same way and that damage causes the mind to default to what is negative. Because of this, the words that go through our mind are vitally important. It is easy for them to be negative, self-defeating words that dig us deeper into the trench. In order to help dig our thoughts out of that default mode and bring light restoration and healing to the brain, we need to make every effort to speak to it in a positive way. Positive words have a powerful effect on the traumatised mind.

Hearing positive words is vital, but speaking them is even more powerful. When we not only think positively but hear ourselves speak out positive declarations, we are taking a further step in affirming and reinforcing the positives to our brains. Speaking the words out loud helps to create a loop from the mouth to the brain, a feedback system. The mouth speaks a positive affirmation, the ears hear it, and the message is received in the brain. Reinforcing this positive message in the brain helps make it easier for you to speak that affirmation out loud again more easily, or other positive affirmations, which in turn go to the ears and to the brain. Listening to positive words from others is good, but hearing our own voice speaking positive words will send a more powerful message to the brain. The brain will recognise that it is *your* voice speaking and 'personalise' what is said, applying it to *you*, *your* mind and *your* body. This is more life-giving than just hearing or thinking positive words.

When you are suffering from trauma it is very hard to speak positive words to yourself but positive self-talk is essential. It may feel strange at first, even alien. When everything about a traumatic situation and its effects is so negative and so bad, positive words don't even seem appropriate. They don't fit. They seem out of place. Our tongues can find it hard to say the words because nothing feels positive at all. When you can't believe in good, it's hard to speak it. If just doesn't feel right.

When others try to speak positively to a traumatised person with words like, 'it will be okay', 'you will get better', 'things will work out', it can be very hard to believe what they say. It can even make you feel angry. Others don't always understand how much you can receive or believe. Traumatised people can be filled with self doubt and loss of confidence in anything good, so people who urge them to see things more positively or speak more positively can be irritating.

You are in Control

However, with self-talk *you* gauge the level. You are in charge of the degree of positivity you can manage. Any positive words will probably always make you feel uncomfortable, but at least you get to decide the level of discomfort you can work with. You are also in charge of the timing. You can start doing this when you feel ready and able. You can also get someone to help. I asked my husband to say brief positive phrases and I repeated them after him. Sometimes it made me angry. If it was a particularly bad day and a bad time, we would stop. But on other days it was very helpful. It was even more helpful if I spoke the words I decided to speak and thought of myself, because I could gauge what I could say and what I could not say.

Positive self-talk is probably the most difficult point of surviving trauma and PTSD. Why? When you are already uncomfortable and in pain, you don't need any more discomfort. You don't want to force yourself to say something good when you are struggling so much to believe it, and just create more pain. That is perfectly understandable. It took me over three years from the time of the trauma to start changing the words PTSD in my life into PRST instead and start believing that I could beat it.

The stress and grief left me with various ailments, countless doctor and hospital visits, a strained marriage, a ragged faith, the many symptoms that come from abusive situations, the inability to engage in our work, and PTSD. It was the self-care techniques that I describe in this book that kept me alive during this period. Much of that time I was alive but barely functioning, but again, it was the techniques in this book that gradually increased my ability to function. Some days just a few positive words of self-talk made the difference between going on with life or contemplating further action to end it all. I could not afford counselling. I was given six free sessions. They helped but what would I do after six weeks were up? In my area the National Health Service waiting list for free counselling and CBT was over two years long. What would I do until then? Every time I seemed to make any headway something else happened to send me spiralling down again. I suffered the excruciating pain of a kidney stone. I had sudden post-menopausal bleeding and ongoing symptoms that wore me down. Extended family members made things worse with lack of support and insensitivity. They had no understanding of trauma. A beloved dog died.

I was lied about to others. I was often so low that the only way I could see was out of life.

It was tough to try and do things to help myself when I was suffering so much. It was very difficult to speak anything positive as everything felt utterly negative and out of control, but even saying one positive thing to myself or about my life, however difficult, could interrupt that negative downward spiral. It may have only been one simple phrase that I could manage but it was something I could control.

The advantage of being in control of the timing and readiness of this is just that: *you* are in control. When everything feels like it has been taken out of your control, it is helpful to be given tools that you control to aid towards your own well-being. Positive words are one of these powerful tools.

The Bridge of Transition

I said this stage can be the most difficult part of surviving trauma. It is the delicate cross-over point from being taken over completely by grief or PTSD, to overtaking grief and PTSD. I say delicate because it feels very fragile. Some days you can speak something positive and use the tools given here, some days it feels like you are taking a step backwards. You can be doing well, and then someone insensitive will say something totally unhelpful and send you plummeting down again, just when you had made a small step. It is so important who you spend time with and I write about that in the section on 'Enjoy Good Company'. There will always be those people who counteract the efforts you are making to survive with ignorance and insensitivity. This cross-over period or transition can also be uncomfortable because speaking positive things when everything is so negative can be very hard to do.

So the transition from being totally controlled by trauma, grief and PTSD to the point of believing and speaking that you can beat it, that you can heal, is a fragile one.

However, it is also a bridge. Each positive belief fed by and founded on positive words is another step on a bridge of hope that can take you to the other side. Each positive thought and word helps the brain to forge a new positive pathway. Damage done can be undone. Each positive thought and word can lift you from the ditch of negative thinking you have been pushed into. You can get out. You can make the climb. On your own terms. In your own way. Positive words and thoughts can be a tool to help you do that.

Positive words and self-talk do not deny what you have experienced. They validate all you have been through and recognise where you are at. However, they help you to take a step from that place in a new direction towards hope and life. They help move you forward to a better place. In fact, you can, over a period of time, move through processes of self-talk which take into account where you are at. Below I list three stages and processes of self-talk you can go through. There are no time limits and you may at times cross from one to the other, depending on what you can cope with and what works best. The aim is to ultimately move forward.

At first, your self-talk might be simple but important validation. I wrote about the importance of validation earlier in the book. Validation recognises and affirms that your response to the trauma you have experienced is normal. A foundation of validation is essential for survival and building on in order to move towards any kind of restoration of the soul.

Here are some examples of positive words of validation. You will find you relate to some of these phrases more than others. Another time, you may find another phrase particularly helpful. It all depends where you are at in your journey. You can speak these out loud to yourself:

(1) Validation

- I have experienced a trauma. The way I feel is normal. I don't like it, but at least I know it is normal. And I know there are others who have felt this way so I am not alone in my feelings.
- Yes, I am experiencing depression. This is not something to be ashamed of. Depression can be a normal result of trauma. I recognise it and I am trying to find ways to help.
- What happened to me was wrong. What they did was wrong. It has affected me and my life. It is not surprising that I feel the way I do.
- I don't want to see people today and it is okay if I don't. It's good for me not to be isolated but today is not a good day for company.
- Right now, I feel like I hate God. I am angry with Him. I feel like He didn't protect me. I feel like He isn't there. These feelings are normal and He understands.
- I am not feeling good today but that is okay. There are good and bad days and a better day will come.

(2) Thankfulness

In the midst of validation self-talk, there are lots of emotions going on that I described at the beginning of the book. Thankfulness is hard, even for small things, when your soul is suffering. If you wish you were dead, you may not be thankful that you are still alive and breathing. But you are. And that is significant. There is purpose and meaning. But those are big words. Learning to be thankful again in just the little things is important, life-giving, and helps the brain in the healing process.

Look up. Look out. Look at yourself in a new way. You may not have everything mentioned here, but express thankfulness for what you do have. Again, some phrases will be more helpful than others. Use these lists in a way that is helpful to you. Add your own things to be thankful for as they come to mind. Remember to speak the words out loud, rather than just think them, to obtain a greater reinforcement of them in your life.
Thankfulness self-talk:

- Thank you for the sky
- Thank you for the warmth of the sun on my face
- Thank you for the touch of rain on my skin
- Thank you for the breeze through the trees
- Thank you for the clouds moving across the sky and the birds flying
- Thank you for the ground under my feet
- Thank you for my feet that faithfully hold me up and walk where I want to go
- Thank you for my hands that work for me all day
- Thank you for my face, my hair, my senses
- Thank you for a roof over my head, a bed to sleep in, for clothes and for food
- Thank you that my brain is working
- Thank you for breath
- Thank you for the people in my life who love me.

(3) *Crossing the Bridge from Negative to Positive*

These words can help you begin the transition from negative thinking and speaking and to cross the bridge into positive thinking and speaking.

- It may not feel like it but somehow I will come through this
- Perhaps I really can heal from PTSD
- PTSD does not have to define me or stay in my life
- I *can* heal from trauma and PTSD
- I don't have to have PTSD. I have...[in this space put your own replacement words]. For example, the letters PTSD could stand for (I am) Peaceful, Thriving, Steady, Determined or (I have) Power, Tenacity, Self-esteem, Dignity
- I will not allow these people/this situation to destroy my life
- I will not be controlled by trauma or PTSD
- My brain can heal from this
- My mind is healing
- My mind is my own and it is my sacred place
- I am valuable, my life is worthwhile
- I have something to give
- I can beat this
- I love myself
- I can heal
- I can.

Faith & Self-talk

If you are a person of faith, this can be helpful with self-talk as you can believe the words of a higher authority, One who is higher and bigger than PTSD, trauma, the current health care techniques for treating trauma, and bigger than your ability to cope. You can speak out words that are above all of those voices. For example:

- God has not given me a spirit of fear, but of power, love, and of a sound mind.[42]
- I have the mind of Christ.[43]
- I don't have to have PTSD. I have P (peace), R (righteousness), S (security), T (triumph).[44] Make up your own words.
- I am strong in the Lord and in the strength of His might.[45]
- God is my refuge and strength.[46]

The Psalms in the Bible are absolutely loaded with words that can be used whether you are going through a time of feeling more negative or positive. Because the Psalms are written from a very real place of experiencing both joy and suffering, triumph and trauma, the words reflect real emotions. Try reading a psalm out loud each day. You will quickly see how real emotions come through the words, that there is validation, thankfulness, and a belief and hope spoken out that is at some place on the bridge of transition from negative to positive.

If faith is damaged or broken by the trauma, this may be hard or impossible. That's okay. As you are able (remember, you are in control), say one brief simple thing. It may feel untrue. It may make you feel angry or uncomfortable. Remember, in all positive self-talk, there is always a measure of discomfort on the bridge from negative to positive, and no less when faith is involved. I had to say positive things even when I didn't feel like I believed what I was saying, just because anything positive would help with my survival more than the repeated and destructive negatives. Over time the words start to grow tiny roots and are able to begin planting themselves in your heart and mind. I talk more about this in the Spiritual Steps.

Don't feel bad when you have bad days. Negative talk will sometimes still invade your speech but you will begin to recognise how different the feeling is between negative and positive talk, and regulate yourself better just because it feels better and you have control of that.

Tool #4 - Meditation

There are different kinds of meditation including spiritual, mindfulness, and mantra meditation.[47] While some approaches seek to empty or disengage the mind, Christian meditation aims to fill the mind with positive thoughts based on scripture as a form of prayer. I do not endorse meditation which focuses on emptying the mind and can lead to dangerous side effects.[48]

Meditation means 'to think, contemplate, devise, ponder.' What you think about and contemplate is very important. When negative thoughts of the traumatic event intrude into your mind, you need to be able to take back the control of your mind.

In trauma, however, and especially with PTSD, it feels like your mind is the main area that is controlling you. Images of the event can intrude on and invade your thinking daily, even several times in an hour, repeatedly revolving around and around, re-traumatising you. It can be exhausting. It is vital for survival to believe that you *can* regain control of your mind and your thoughts. And you can. It may take time. It will take some effort. But you really can. But how?

Words are a crucial tool. Thinking positive words, speaking them, muttering them, whispering them, reading them, are all forms of meditation. Words create either positive or negative images in our minds. With meditation, we choose what to meditate on. Meditation helps you to replace intrusive, involuntary, negative thoughts and images with purposefully chosen and controlled thoughts, images and words.

When negative thoughts and images suddenly grab you and seem to take control and demand your attention, you need something simple you can do immediately to put the focus onto something else. Focusing your mind on an object in the near distance can help. As you contemplate the shape, colour, light, material of the object, your mind is being retrained to pay attention to you and what you decide to focus on. At the same time, you can reflect on how your body is feeling as you look at the object, feel your weight in the seat on which you are sitting, feel the position of your body and relax your muscles. What are your hands doing? What are your legs doing? How is your breathing? Let your breathing become slower and deeper. As you relax more, you can again focus on the object. This kind of 'meditation' helps you to regain awareness, retrain your mind, and regain a calmer, more controlled, more stable emotional and mental state.

Don't Freewheel

As human beings we are usually meditating on something throughout the day. If you could stop yourself periodically throughout the day and make a note of what you are thinking about, you will find your mind is never empty. You are usually thinking about someone or something, something that was said, a situation, a feeling, either positive or negative. In fact, we are so used to thinking involuntarily that we are capable of allowing our minds to just go into 'neutral' and 'free-wheel', thinking about what they want when they want to. This is even more so when we have experienced a traumatic event. Unless you focus the mind, it will revolve the traumatic event around and around in your thinking without your permission. Meditation fills your mind with something else to focus on. That's why listening to positive words on a computer such as motivational videos, helpful music, scriptures, stories, informative radio programmes, or hearing our own voices speaking positive words are all so helpful.

Meditation does not have to be religious, but it can be. It does not have to be in a certain position but can be done in a relaxed position and state. Meditation can also happen as we go about our everyday lives. Using controlled deep breathing can help a person to gain a state of relaxation and focus the mind.

In trauma, you can see how meditation is using positive replacement and self-talk to put you in control of your mind and well-being. You can use some of the self-talk words and phrases I included on pages 97-98 in your meditation, contemplating them as thoughts, dwelling on them, letting them roll around in your mind and heart, and speaking them to yourself.

Dreams

So, you are employing some of the methods here to deal with troublesome images and you find that you can go for a couple of days feeling a little better. Then suddenly, you are 'hit' by a bad dream. In that dream are exactly the images you are trying to get rid of. In the dream, however, they are not just still images, they are moving pictures, a movie playing out in your mind that takes you into its story like a character in a play. Suddenly you are right there, involved in the drama. And as dreams do, it takes you into new angles on the drama, the trauma coming out in new ways.

This is exactly what happened to me. After betrayal, lies and abandonment that left me with PTSD, I would fight the daily battle until I was able to experience a few days in a row of feeling a little better and on a more even keel. Then I would be hit hard by a very vivid dream in which I was an unwilling participant. In the dream, I was searching for the betrayer, desperate to talk some sense into them. When I found them, however, they were hard, cold and remorseless, as if they were another person, completely blind and deceived. I tried and tried but nothing worked. And then I became so incredibly angry I shook and shook them.

Thankfully, it was just a dream, but when I woke up I felt like I was in another world, my head spinning, trying to grab hold of the true reality. My emotions were spent and raw. It could take me a couple of days to recover from dreams like that.

Dreams that replay, embellish, or express what you have been through can be a way for the mind to try and outwork the trauma and seek to release the depth of some of the emotions you feel. However, they can end up setting you back so that you feel you have to start again at finding some peace and equilibrium. That can be draining and discouraging.

There are some methods you can employ to help. Firstly, realising this can happen and is normal is an important step. If you are armed with that knowledge you are a step forward already.

Secondly, on the day after a dream like that, be gentle with yourself. You may feel irritable, frustrated, bad-tempered and tired. Find something to do that you enjoy, spend time with people you like being around, have a soothing bath, and just generally do things that soothe ragged emotions. It may take a day or two, but the emotions will begin to subside. Continue to employ methods of dealing with troubling images instead of letting the images from the dream trouble you.

Thirdly, there are a couple of methods you can learn to use while you are having the dream. Yes, there are even things you can learn to do in your sleep.

As a child I would have bad dreams about falling from a great height and knowing any moment I was going to hit the ground. The fall itself was horrid but the anticipation of hitting the ground was even worse. When I did finally hit, the sensation made me feel sick and strange. The experience was very unpleasant but happened quite often. In the end, I got so used to the dream that I developed a coping strategy. I found I was able to infiltrate and control the events and outcome of a dream, instead of being controlled by it and being taken where I did not want to go. I began to learn what it felt like to be entering into a part of a dream that was going to turn into something nasty or negative. I recognised certain images, feelings, places, peoples, and situations I had seen before in previous bad dreams. Before the dream had a chance to turn into something dark or bad, I did something different to change the outcome. In the dream I walked out of that room. I said 'no' and walked away from the people. I didn't go to the high buildings where I might fall. Or, I switched the dream off altogether and started thinking about something completely different and more pleasant. I changed 'dream channel'. I learned to do this without even waking up fully and it made a big difference to my 'dream life'. At last, I felt I could be safer in my dreams.

Another method I learned was to wake myself up. If I was falling and about to hit the ground in my dream, I made myself wake up before I did so it couldn't happen. Then I learned to wake myself up before other negative events too.

Your brain has some marvellous safety features that can protect you in your sleep. You can learn to have greater control over the outcome of dreams by changing the situation in your dream, changing the dream, or waking yourself before something happens.

The ability to change situations and outcomes in your dream is one form of what is known as 'lucid' dreaming or knowing that you are dreaming while in the dream state.[49] It enables you to have greater decision-making function about what will happen in the dream. This ability can be attained through therapy where the therapist will ask the person to work out an alternative scenario they want to happen in a dream. Closing their eyes, the person rehearses an enactment of a different outcome in their imagination. This can help people create a mastery dream that overrules the traumatic dream.

If you are having bad, repetitive, post-traumatic nightmares, you might find this kind of therapy helpful. Some people learn to do this without therapy. If you feel consistently unsafe in certain dreams, you may be able to learn how to recognise a potentially unsafe situation within a dream. You may be able to then change the outcome yourself by imagining and rehearsing a different scenario while awake, and outworking it while in the dream state.

Just knowing this is possible can be a step towards changing the outcome of bad dreams, by replacing them with an imagery you would prefer.

Repeated traumatic events that occur in dreams can also teach you to wake yourself up before the bad things happen. This is a safety mechanism. Years of traumatic dreams finally taught me how to employ this method as a way of protecting myself and keeping sleep as a positive experience. You may find you naturally learn that ability over time too as a form of self-protection. You can also see a therapist to help you in this area.

5. Enjoy Good Company

When you have suffered trauma, you may well want to be alone, and there is nothing wrong with that as long as it is helpful to you. However, I do encourage you not to isolate yourself. You need to enjoy good company. I say *good* company because some company will not be helpful. You need to choose your company to ensure you are with people who will do you good. Be around people with whom you feel safe. That is very important for your well-being.

Do not spend time around people who will make you feel depressed or anxious with morbid stories, tales of woe, and lists of troubling and anxiety-producing events, or who will encourage substance abuse. That will not be helpful as it will traumatise you more and tire your mind. Equally, you may not find it helpful to be around extremely positive, happy-clappy people who only highlight the misery you feel.

Some people are ignorant of the effects of trauma and will be good at making glib remarks such as, "Isn't it time to move on?" or keep telling you they know how you feel when they don't, overwhelm you with their own personal story, or play down your experience with comments like, "Surely it's not that bad?". There will always be unhelpful and insensitive people but you don't need to spend your time around them. Spend time with people who are good for you, who are understanding, show grace, who are willing to talk, who make you laugh, make you feel safe, comfortable and happy, but who also distract you and draw you out of yourself so that when you are with them you can have some respite from the intensity of negative feelings.

You need family, friends and social gatherings as a natural support group. It may also be helpful to be with others going through trauma themselves if you can use that situation as a platform for constructive sharing, to help yourself put things in perspective by remembering you are not the only one, and perhaps helping to provide mutual comfort and understanding for someone else.

Good company helps restore joy, gives support and encouragement, can take your mind off things, bring laughter into your world, and provide distractions. Get together with people with whom you can do an activity like art, play a sport, discuss a topic of interest together, do a project, and have fun.

Seeing a counsellor can be very beneficial and is very important for those suffering PTSD or C-PTSD. These visits can provide you with helpful company for a brief period of time at regular intervals, get you out, help you gain new perspectives, and provide necessary tools for your well-being. Make sure, however, that the counsellor's approach works for you. For example, talk therapy can be useful for some. For others however, it might not be helpful to keep rehashing your story. A trained counsellor should be sensitive to this.

Reliving a story over and over again with anyone who takes an interest can sometimes re-traumatise the person. That said, never be afraid to talk to someone about what you have experienced. It is important that traumatic events are shared especially if there is abuse involved. Never let anyone prevent you from sharing about abusive situations. Silencing people who are being abused or who have suffered abuse is simply another form of abuse. People who try to make you keep quiet about abuse or the trauma of abuse are dangerous. In these events, always find a safe person to talk to.

If you come from a culture that makes it difficult to share the trauma you have been through and its effects on you, you are likely to bottle it all up inside. You should not have to deal with so much pain alone. It is not healthy to do so. Being able to talk about what you have experienced is important and not something to be ashamed of. You will need to focus on doing what is healthy, not on pleasing others. Don't be afraid to share with someone and get the help you need.

Of course, you will need time by yourself too. This is very important for restoration and healing. Don't spend so much time with others that when you are by yourself you are depressed because you are alone. Have creative and constructive things you can focus on when you are by yourself. I wrote this book during just such a time. If you are a person of faith, get time alone with God. Take time to settle your mind and heart, vent and express your feelings, talk, make your complaints, pray, speak His Word. Take time alone to do whatever you need to do without self-consciousness, with no-one watching or listening.

The Marriage Relationship

Trauma can have a significant and lasting impact on the marriage relationship. One or both partners may be experiencing the direct effects of trauma. If it is both partners, the effects may be at different levels. This may depend on the nature of the trauma, how it affects the man and woman differently, how it affects the different personalities, the difference in histories and any previous experience of childhood trauma in either spouse, and the subsequent available coping capacity.

If one partner only is directly affected by trauma, the other partner can suffer the secondary effects of the trauma on their spouse. For example, if the partner who has been traumatised is suffering from anxiety, depression, and or symptoms of Post Traumatic Stress Disorder, this will change their behaviour. This will obviously impact the non-traumatised spouse. In this way, the non-traumatised spouse is experiencing secondary effects of the trauma.

Depression, emotional turmoil, grief, crises of faith, anger and other issues can all make it seem like your partner has become a different person. They are not a different person, of course. They are the same person you loved and appreciated, but trauma can impact thinking, perceptions, self-esteem, confidence, emotions and behaviours to the degree that it feels like they have changed into someone else. Trauma can also have a negative impact on health bringing even more difficult dynamics to deal with and adding extra stress.

The stress of trauma, loss, and a change in your relationship can put huge strain on a marriage. This can lead to further secondary traumas. Sustaining the relationship can become more difficult. This can ultimately lead to separation and divorce, both of which are also painful and traumatic events, especially when children are involved. In this way, trauma can expand outwards, seeming to multiply itself, affecting more and more lives.

It is so important to recognise what is going on in your marriage relationship, and to try to learn and understand as much as possible. Learning about how trauma works, and how it may have affected your spouse, can give you both tools to find the best ways to manage the situation and create more positive outcomes.

I know this from my own experience. The trauma we experienced as a couple and as a family was ongoing. It was not just a one-off event. It left us in a state of *not knowing*, of grief and loss, of pain in our family year after year. The stress impacted me more than my husband due to personality and less coping capacity available due to childhood and previous traumas. This meant that I was the one whose behaviour changed. It was also *my* health that was negatively impacted. The anger, grief, depression and stress-related health issues naturally affected his life too. As I was experiencing menopause at exactly the same time as the trauma, this gave us twice the burden to deal with.

The impact on our marriage was huge. Like any marriage, we had issues to deal with already, but at least those were the ones we were familiar with and brought stresses that we could creatively manage through constructive conversation and change. However, when trauma hit, it ramped stress up to extraordinary levels that frequently brought our relationship to dangerous edges.

Trauma will most certainly put you in a position of needing to decide how to proceed in your relationship in a way that is as constructive as possible. The last thing either of you need is more trauma added to your lives. Now is not the time to make big decisions that end in divorce, that impact the rest of the family even more, and that bring further trauma to you and others.

Trauma can either cause your marriage to become a disaster area or become a source of support. There will come a point when you will need to make a decision what it is to be. Making the decision for your marriage to be a source of support for each other does not mean it will always be easy. There will be many times when the stress of the trauma overwhelms your decision and you find yourselves back in a bad place again. However, with your growing knowledge and experience of trauma-related effects and how to deal with them, and your decision to support one another, you can come through those difficult times, shortening their duration, and learn how to return to a more supportive situation more quickly.

The part of the brain that deals with good judgement and decision-making can be impaired in trauma. That is why it is good not to act hastily and make decisions based in anger or on fight or flight responses when dealing with important and big issues such as your marriage.

Constructive Support

Here are some simple ways you can be constructive and supportive in your marriage instead of responding to the destructive feelings of trauma:

Do something calming and relaxing. Instead of packing bags, walking out the door and leaving, go for a walk somewhere that calms your mind and soul, allows you to take deep breaths and think more carefully, and helps you return home in a more constructive frame of mind.

Offer to put the kettle on, sit down and have a cup of tea. You would be amazed at the positive psychological effect that simple act can have on stressed people, and how it can potentially diffuse a situation and give opportunity for discussion instead.

Love. If a traumatised person is suffering badly, crying, angry, reliving events, shouting, directing anger at you, God and the world, talking negatively or being self-destructive, love them. Sometimes, just taking the person in your arms and saying how sorry you are that they are suffering can bring the stress levels down. Understanding can be a powerful support. (I am not talking about clear and immediate danger from suicide or physical self-harm. If that is evident, getting help quickly is important.)

Spontaneity. Make spontaneous suggestions such as, 'Let's go for a walk together', 'Let's go out and eat'. Do something that takes you both out of the environment and the situation. If you can't get out of the environment, get something out of the environment! Put a movie, show or comedy on to watch together. Change room. Play some music. Arrange to talk with someone online. Cook a meal. Suggest doing something right then that you will both enjoy and takes your mind off the immediate stresses.

Learn. Learn from books (such as this one). Learn online. Learn from others. Learn about the effects of trauma and learn to recognise them in your partner. It may not always be a good idea to remind them that they are just responding to the effects of trauma when they are having a crisis! They may or may not thank you for it! If they respond well to that reminder that is good. If they do not, taking them out of the situation to do something they enjoy is another solution.

Remember what you have learned. It is very important to remember what you learn about how trauma affects people and to use the tools you are given. Putting into practice what you learn is vital. Write down the steps you can take and the constructive responses you can have and put the list somewhere accessible that you can refer to in times of need.

Discuss solutions. On more positive days, talk together about how you can better support each other. You won't always put it all into practice in a crisis, but you can improve over time.

Patience. A great deal of patience is needed towards each other when dealing with the effects of trauma. Being patient is often the last thing you want to be! However, as you grow in your understanding of how trauma affects people, you can build compassion and patience. Practise using constructive responses with each other will also help build greater endurance and patience.

A safe place. Traumatised people need safety and security. Your marriage can at least provide for you both a familiar, and hopefully relatively known and safe place in a time of trauma, loss and change. It is worth working with each other to provide and improve that needed safe place. Discuss ways that you can make your relationship, marriage and life circumstances feel safer for each other.

Step in and help. In trauma, a person's normal energy levels can be affected so that fulfilling the usual daily tasks is more tiring and overwhelms them more quickly. Being observant to notice when activities are overloading the other person is a good idea. Being ready to step in and take over the task or offering to do a job to take the pressure off them can be a great relief and make the difference between a good or bad day.

Have fun. I cannot emphasise enough the importance of just having fun together and laughing together. Find things to do that you both enjoy and that take your mind off the stresses even for short moments. Learn to do those activities together more often. Make the fun times longer. Replace as many of the potential hours and days of stress possible with enjoyable activities instead. We enjoyed walking on the beach, walking and romping with our dogs, doing jigsaws, gardening, collecting shells, eating out, going to local country dances and having fun with other people, reading out loud, making work systems at home function better, working on projects together, discussing

114

future plans, and having those inevitable British cups of tea. Those and other simple things didn't take the pain away, but they helped us get through the days and the years, brought joy into our relationship, and helped keep our marriage going when all hell was bent on destroying it. We decided to support each other. We did not want to allow the trauma to cause us to throw away thirty years of marriage.

Get help. Do not be ashamed to get help individually or together from a trauma-trained counsellor who you can talk with. Talking with someone else can help relieve the pressure on both you and your spouse, and help you work out and put into practice better strategies for survival and support for each other.

Self and other care. Keep caring for yourself. Caring for yourself also values your partner. Taking the time to make yourself look nice makes you feel better and makes them feel valued. Visit the hairdresser and have a relaxing time getting your hair done. It will benefit both of you. Go together. Go shopping together and buy something new to wear. Buy a new cologne or fragrance and smell nice for each other. All of these little elements of caring for your self make a difference in marriage at any time, but especially in trauma.

At the same time, if your partner is having a terrible time caring for themselves and feels a wreck, don't belittle their appearance. Help them care for themselves. On the mornings when I could not get up, my husband helped me get dressed. I hated being so dependent on him, but once I was up, I was thankful he helped me start my day. He took on the preparation of the evening meal. After years of doing most of the cooking myself, that was a real help and blessing. Look for ways to express extra care for yourself and your partner.

Sleep is a form of care for both partners, whether it is ensuring you get enough yourself, or helping the other person to get enough. Lack of sleep and over-tiredness during trauma can be the 'straw that breaks the camel's back' in a relationship, burning out already frazzled emotional resources. To help maintain your marriage and be supportive of each other, ensure you are both getting the sleep you need. Giving someone a chance to nap in the day, sleep longer in the morning, or enabling and encouraging them to get to bed earlier can make a significant difference.

Pray together. When a crisis of faith has taken place, the last thing people of faith might feel like doing is praying together. I talk more about the feelings involved in this in the Spiritual Steps. However, in the context of a marriage relationship where people of faith are involved, prayer is crucial. It doesn't have to be long. It doesn't have to be flowery or sound spiritual. It is just important to maintain that spiritual dynamic as a couple in connecting in prayer with each other and with God.

If both of you are struggling spiritually, someone will still need to take the lead in this. It can help to just have something you can read out loud to each other, a scripture, a Psalm, a prayer written down, something where you don't have to think too hard. Or you may find it helpful to pray together with someone else. In either case, you may feel very unspiritual at first. You may lack trust in the God and in the Scriptures which you so readily prayed before the trauma. Your anger may make your words of prayer feel bitter. In his excellent book, *When Heaven Is Silent*, Ronald Dunn talks about a lady who was going through trauma. She asked him this question,

'What do you do when you don't know what to do?'
His response was,
'Do what you know to do.'

When you don't know what to do, do what you know to do and do it anyway. These are excellent words and they apply to many things we do in life. If you don't know what to do in the trauma, do what you know to do. Get dressed. Eat. Feed the dog. Do the shopping. Do the things you know to do. If you know that prayer is important, pray. If you can't pray like you did before, find a new way to pray but pray anyway. And pray together. At first, praying with Stuart made me angry. I argued with his prayers. I argued the Scriptures. I argued with God. But I realised I wasn't doing myself any good at all. If anything, I was only making everything worse. When you don't feel like praying, pray anyway, and pray together. It may feel stilted at first, but it will begin to feel normal again and it will do you good.

The other response to prayer is to just not do it and ignore it and all spiritual things completely, to put God on a shelf somewhere in disgust and disappointment. But that will not work in relieving trauma and helping your relationship. People of faith know better than that. Ignoring what you know will not help ultimately. Ignoring God as a couple will not help your faith, nor will it help you come through the most difficult season of your life together. Prayer turns your life as a couple into a three-strand cord. It involves God. It softens hearts. It connects you. It keeps you on the right track. It works gently on restoration. And eventually it will start to renew your relationships and bring hope.

Sex

Sex can take a nose-dive when in trauma. However, it can be a healing and comforting activity with your spouse or faithful partner at this time. I say sex within a marriage relationship or with a faithful partner because studies show that sex in a long-term, faithful relationship as a married couple has the most beneficial results.[50] Of course, I recognise not everyone is married, but sex with a faithful partner would be the next best thing, although not as good according to research. In either case, I am referring to loving, considerate, supportive relationships where trust and care are a priority. Engaging in one-night stands, short-term, insecure relationships, or sex just to feel good doesn't have the same benefits in relieving stress long-term.

Trauma can decrease libido (sexual desire), and the depression that can accompany Post Traumatic Stress Disorder can leave you feeling like sex is a good idea for which you just can't find the motivation or energy. If you have been traumatised by some kind of sexual abuse, perhaps sex makes you feel taken advantage of, even by the one you love. The last thing you and your partner need is more stress. Be affectionate in small ways by hugging, holding hands, little kisses here and there, kind acts done for each other. In bed, hold each other before you go to sleep, no expectations, no condemnation, rebuilding trust, however long it takes. Eventually, something sexual will stir. It may not happen as often as you would both like, but it can happen. Occasional is better than nothing at all. If you have suffered sexual abuse that continues to negatively affect your sex life, try to get counselling from a specialist in this area, even just a few sessions if money is an issue. Even a few sessions can give you tools and a new perspective and you can learn new approaches and attitudes as a couple to help things work.

When you do have intercourse, or even just enjoy foreplay, feel-good chemicals will be released into your system that are a positive help on your healing journey. Sex is something you can enjoy as much as you want with your partner in any form that is comfortable to you (and moral), and that is beneficial to your physical, mental and emotional well-being. This will be good for your marriage at a time of stress.

Menopause & Trauma

I would like to say a brief but special word to women who are experiencing menopause and trauma at the same time.

My periods ended and I started experiencing hot flushes at exactly the same time that our family trauma occurred. I didn't know initially that the hot flushes were related to menopause. I had suffered hyperthyroidism for years and thought that the sudden rushes of heat and anxiety were a hyperthyroid 'storm' where the thyroid significantly over-functions causing discomfort and distress. As I learned that I was rapidly moving to being post-menopausal, more traumatic events happened. Now I was experiencing trauma in our family, work and health at the same time as significant menopause symptoms. All these major traumas happened at once, and it continued over the next few months and years. Trauma and menopause at the same time are not a good combination.

For some women, menopause, its implications, the hormonal, body and mood changes, and associated symptoms such as hot flushes and weight gain are already traumatic. Experiencing a major life trauma at the same time can be more than any normal person can bear. The continual fluctuations in hormones and the decrease in estrogen and progesterone means you are dealing with chemical changes and their effects which are hard to control and make dealing with trauma even more difficult.

That is exactly what happened to me and the sheer immensity and daily overload of what I needed to cope with in being post-menopausal and experiencing C-PTSD led me on a particularly bad day to call a helpline just to talk to someone. Thankfully, while I could not afford ongoing counselling, I was able to get six free counselling sessions and at least a few paid sessions. That did help. If you are suffering an overload of both menopause and trauma at the same time, I do recommend getting all the help you can.

You will need to make decisions about what kind of help you want to proceed with. Do you want to minimize the hot flushes and other symptoms first? Will easing menopause symptoms be sufficient to help make the trauma effects easier to manage? Will you opt to deal with the trauma effects first in the hope that it will help you manage the menopause symptoms better? Will you take a two-pronged approach and try to improve both areas at the same time? Will you look for natural approaches, simply use what modern medicine has to offer, or combine the two? It is worth finding out about medical options from a doctor familiar with hormonal issues. Even better is to find a doctor who understands the impact of trauma and menopause together. Some anti-depressants can help control both the hot flushes and the depression. There are also natural approaches to both depression and menopause symptoms. It is worth doing some research and trying some different approaches to see what works for you in the healthiest way. That will all take some time, of course, so remember that there is not a one-pill, quick-fix cure. Be ready to take the time necessary to find out what works for you to help you survive and manage this season of life.

All women are different, their menopause experience is different, and the way they respond to various treatments and therapies is different. It will be a process of discovery.

It is helpful to be able to pull back and take a look at life and say, 'What is this season of life encouraging me to do?' There is no doubt that menopause by itself is urging us as women to rethink *you* and discover the new *you* that wants to emerge. What does it mean for you? What do you want to get from this time in your life? What do you want to achieve in life? Who do you want to be? When you experience menopause and trauma at the same time, the questions take on an even more significant importance. Adding trauma to menopause can make life feel like it is at an end for you. In reality, in the lucid moments when we get a glimpse through the clouds that have covered us, we are being encouraged to ask this question, 'What now?' Trauma has happened. Menopause has happened. It may feel like the worst time of your life. The 'What Now?' question gives us hope that this is not actually an end but a beginning. It may turn out to be the biggest beginning we will experience as an older woman, a kind of rebirth when we finally stop long enough to ask the most important questions, to find out what is truly important to us, and instead of just fulfilling the needs of others, we finally start looking at fulfilling some of our own.

This is a vital time to care for and love *yourself*. The emotional stress of trauma can make menopause symptoms worse, and the symptom of menopause can make the emotional stress of trauma worse. Women can naturally be very sacrificial, putting their needs last even to the point of hurting or sabotaging themselves. I urge you not to do that but to relieve pressure on yourself by making some things easier and less stressful for you. It is essential to do all that is possible to ease the stress of trauma and make your life simpler, easier and more enjoyable. The tools in this book will be useful for this. It is not possible to give timescales, but over time, learning to cope with menopause and trauma can get better and it can become more manageable.

There are conventional and natural treatments for symptoms so do find out about these and do all you can to help yourself in a way that feels right for you.

Animal-Assisted Therapy

There is another kind of therapy and company that can be very helpful. I am talking about the company of animals. Animal-Assisted-Therapy & Activities (AAT & AAA) is another growing form of therapy being used to help many different kinds of people of all ages and situations in life.

I am trained in Animal-Assisted-Therapy (AAT) & Activities (AAA) and used my trained therapy dog to work with orphaned children in Thailand. These children had been traumatised as babies or very young children and had difficulty trusting people. I was asked to use AAT & AAA to work on their emotional development. I used my therapy dog, baby rabbits and ducks. The children grew in confidence, trust, and new skills, and the results were beneficial. Equine therapy (using horses) is very popular, and I know a lady who uses two hairy pigs to help people in her counselling sessions. People are also finding positive results from chickens and other birds and animals. Therapy animals are being used in hospitals and elderly people's homes, in counselling sessions, equine therapy centres, and therapy 'farms' where you can go to visit the animals and get involved in their care.

If you have a pet, they can be a valuable source of comfort and love. The love of animals is unconditional.

Stroking them is another way to release feel-good chemicals in the body and reduce stress. The routines of feeding, grooming and caring for animals provide healthy structure for people in trauma, grief and depression, and PTSD. Caring for another creature can help you to get your mind off yourself and onto something else, and soften and soothe a hurting heart.

My rough collie dog, Ruby, proved to be a huge help during trauma. Each day, I walked her around the land where we lived taking a ball of my knotted-up old socks with me. She never liked plastic toys of any kind, but she loved that ball of socks. We played 'find it' as I hid it behind me, played fetch, fought over it in the most ridiculous ways, all of which was great fun and made me laugh and act like a little girl. Grooming her long fur is very therapeutic and letting her lick my feet is surprisingly comforting. It sounds disgusting but it was a way she could groom me in return, and I enjoyed the gentle attention and found it tickled and made me laugh too. On tough days, I have often buried my head in my dogs' fur and just breathed along with them, stared into their eyes and found unconditional love. As long as they are well, they wake up happy, are never depressed, want routines, make us laugh, and are always the same. All these things are good for trauma and grief. Animals are a gift.

If you don't have your own animal(s), there are more and more places being set up for the sole purpose of giving people the opportunity to engage with animals. This is especially important for those in urban settings who have little opportunity or space for a pet or to spend time around domesticated animals. If you ask a relative to look into it for you, ask a pastor, or just look and ask around via friends and the internet, you will find something. Perhaps someone could take you for a visit once a week. You may even fall in love with an animal and become a sponsor, enjoying the benefits but not being responsible for full-time care.

That said, if at this time of your life you find the stress and anger you are dealing with causes you to feel or be abusive towards or neglectful of an animal, please take constructive steps to help yourself and your animal friend and ask someone else to look after them for you at this time. You could visit them to reassure yourself they are safe and still yours. You could engage with care routines, but the sole responsibility of care would not be on you full-time.

During times of trauma and PTSD, you will be particularly vulnerable and the thought of getting a pet might be tempting for you. Sometimes this proves to be exactly what a person needs. The company of the right dog, cat, or other animal can make a tremendous difference to a person's life, restoring meaning and purpose. However, make sure you think through this carefully, and preferably in conjunction with others who know you and what you are going through so you can make a wise decision. For example, this may not be the time for you to take on a young puppy requiring training including potty training, exercise, feeding etc. You might want to get an older rescue dog. However, rescue dogs, while sometimes saving the day for suffering people, can also have unpredictable problems of their own which might be difficult for you to cope with. What I am saying is, don't rush into a decision that involves the life of another creature and puts them at risk and you in danger of further burden, stress and guilt. Think through the decision carefully and talk with others who may be able to help you make the right match.

6. Make a Change

During a time of trauma or when suffering from PTSD, it is not always a good idea to make big decisions and changes. Your judgment can be impaired at this time and you don't want to make decisions that you might regret. Also, if you are receiving counselling or other treatment and help, you don't necessarily want to make changes that will cause you to have to change your treatment provider. That is a big upheaval and could upset the routines and provision that are so necessary for you at this time.

Sometimes, however, some kinds of change are helpful when you are suffering from trauma. They can help you get away from past memories, bad friendships, abusive situations, and people and places that might cause flashbacks or re-traumatise you. Avoidance of certain situations can be a sign that you are suffering from PTSD. There is treatment you can receive that helps you to face those people, places, reminders and triggers that you are avoiding so that they don't have such a negative effect on you. That may be an important part of your healing. At other times, it may also be good to make changes to your life so you don't have to keep dealing with them. In other words, it may not be a necessary part of life or healing to have to face or live with those things or people that trigger negative responses in you.

When I experienced a spiritually abusive event from controlling leaders in a church in the UK, I suffered with depression for the ensuing three and a half years. I didn't know so much about trauma back then and did not seek out help. I tried to manage the situation myself and deal with the 'bogey men' that had come into my life, while being regularly faced with them. I kept going to that church every Sunday in the belief that I could bravely face up to the abuse that had occurred. I thought I was strong enough not to be affected by it, to refuse to allow it to affect my life. I felt that if I had truly forgiven that person, I would not have a problem continuing to be a part of that church group. In reality, every Sunday was a miserable torment that made me cry and re-traumatised me as I endured the abuser's praise ministry, and listened to teaching given by other leaders who had allowed it to happen and given no support. It was a tough job having to be so strong all the time and the reality is that constantly facing the people and place where the trauma happened was really doing me no good. It was not essential for me to keep going to that particular church. I *did* have a choice.

In the end, I made a choice for my own well-being. We moved away from that situation with our work to another country. We had lived and worked in Asia for many years previously. We already had friends there and experience of living in that culture so it wasn't entirely new. Having things that were familiar was helpful. Leaving the memories, the damaging people and places behind gave me a new lease of life. The pain disappeared. I was able to enjoy the new things and the old friends. Although it meant starting again, I didn't mind because I felt better.

Seven years later, the person who had been abusive contacted me and apologised for what they had done. I had already forgiven them, but moving away dealt with the residual pain and prevented me from being re-traumatised by memories and life in the environment where the abuse took place.

Moving is, of course, a big change to make. Moving creates its own stresses which may not be ones you need right now. But perhaps there are other changes you could make. If certain places you visit make you struggle with sadness and make life difficult every time you go there, don't go for a while. If pain is triggered by being around people who might be hurt by your absence, you can say you need a temporary break while you heal. You can explain why or get someone to do that for you. You can visit some new places. You can take up a new hobby.

Making positive lifestyle changes is always a good idea. Get help for addictions and dependencies and learn to find other constructive coping mechanisms. If the friendships you have are unhelpful for healing from trauma, find some new friends you can spend time with who do you good. You don't have to move, but you could take some time away somewhere. A vacation by the sea, a few days with a friend at a ranch riding horses, some time on a farm connecting with the animals and nature, a stay with a friend in a quiet cabin in the woods hearing the sounds of the birds in the morning and the crickets at night – a change can sometimes be a beneficial rest from all that is too familiar.

Even changing routines, changing your furniture around, redecorating a room, changing the function of a room into a place where you can do some creative projects, sorting out stuff you don't need anymore and clearing things out, can all be therapeutic and give you a sense of newness and freshness which is beneficial.

7. Nurture Feelings of Well-being

When we have suffered a trauma, the whole of life can feel different. It can feel unsafe, unprotected, threatening, and you can feel uncared for and unable to care for yourself.

It's easy to nurture the negative emotions, images, fears, and regrets. It's no effort at all to allow these to play on our mind and hearts twenty-four hours a day, taking over our lives and consuming our creativity and energy.

As we find coping mechanisms, there will be moments when we are able to get on with life and put positive things into our lives. During those times, we will experience some positive feelings of well-being. They may be tentative and fragile, but these moments remind us what it is like to feel better, to feel well, to feel something like our normal selves. Perhaps we get a visit from a good friend who brings light into our lives. Perhaps we start a new activity that engages our minds and hands, that distracts us from the trouble for a while and gives us a sense of well-being, pleasure, and enjoyment. Perhaps a walk in nature gives us some respite from the pain as we breathe fresh air, enjoy sunshine, beautiful views and wildlife. Perhaps we release some tension playing a sport. These may be brief moments in the scale of the daily trauma, but they are like jewels shining in a dark place, and oases in a desert.

One day these words came to me, 'Nurture feelings of well-being.' It's the feelings of positive emotions created in these moments, however brief, that need to be remembered and nurtured. If doing a particular constructive activity gives you a sense of well-being, do more of it. Later, or on another day, recall the healthy emotions that were created, remember them, enjoy them, and bask in them. As you do this you nurture and feed the positive emotions, helping them re-emerge, gain ground and grow. Don't let anyone make you feel guilty about doing healthy things that nurture those feelings of well-being.

Alternative Therapies & Touch

Alternative therapies and touch can be wonderful ways to nurture feelings of well-being and remind ourselves what it feels like to feel calm and relaxed.

Alternative 'touch' therapies such as reflexology, non-contact therapeutic touch (touch therapy), and things like 'tapping', while not scientifically proven, have proved helpful for some. Others might find them a bit odd, and some people would struggle with the possibility of related spiritual or occult activity. However, what is certain is that our bodies and minds do respond to the positive power of human presence and touch. Receiving a 'therapy' puts a person into a relaxed atmosphere in a pleasant setting where the focus is solely on them and their well-being. Sometimes there is music playing. The therapist is present and gentle. The touch on the body is soothing, comforting, relaxing, and restorative. That in itself brings about positive responses in our bodies and souls.

Massage therapy is marvellous for producing all those feelings while at the same time addressing very specific areas of tension created in the body by stress. I have found massage therapy particularly helpful when my daughter has done it for me, and especially stress-relieving knowing that she was doing it for me at no charge! Personally, I would recommend a trained massage therapist like my daughter who can provide a soothing atmosphere combined with professionalism to recognise specific needs. This can be expensive, but even if it is once every couple of months or so, it is something to look forward to. In case you are under the impression that I had the advantage of regular free massages, unfortunately, I didn't. It would have been nice, but for years we lived thousands of miles away from our daughter, so these massages only happened occasionally when we got to see her.

Self-Therapy & Touch

Our bodies can become very neglected. We stuff food in, go through our standard routines of washing, dressing, daily activities, work, sitting, getting ready for bed and finally sleeping before starting another day. But how much do we actually actively love our bodies and affirm them? We may have a significant other in our lives, or close family members with whom we can experience a greater sense of touch through hugging and affection, lovemaking with a spouse, or a friend's hand of comfort on our shoulder. But what about engaging with our own bodies ourselves? We can all too often give ourselves a critical eye in the mirror, complain about how our body looks and feels, and take it for granted. Our souls, consisting of our mind, will and emotions, are often neglected too, caught up in busyness, running on empty, just functioning and reacting to circumstances. How often do we acknowledge them and respect the needs of our soul? Sometimes, and I believe especially in trauma, we need to make a point of affirming and loving ourselves, soul and body.

Hug Yourself

At various times on my journey with trauma, I found it

helpful to hug myself. I simply wrapped my arms around my own shoulders and hugged myself. I dwelt in that moment, speaking words of love and affirmation to myself, 'I love you. You are loved. You are beautiful. I appreciate you. Don't worry. Somehow it will be alright. Somehow, *you* will be alright.' In lonely and despairing moments, it has been surprisingly therapeutic, calming and reassuring. Try it.

Speak to Your Body

Life itself can cause a disconnection between body and soul. We get used to the disconnect and it can get difficult to know how to bring body and soul back into harmony with each other, recognising each other, acknowledging each other, loving and appreciating each other.

That might sound odd to some people but let me give you an example. How often do you thank your feet? My mother loved her feet. She would soak them in a bowl of warm water at the end of the day and put cream on them. They were not very attractive feet. They were like mine, short and wide with stubby toes, but she never criticised them. Years before, in her youth, they had been put into ballet pointe shoes until she suffered a knee injury and had to give up dancing. Those feet had ridden horses. They had carried her many miles. They didn't need to be beautiful feet for her to appreciate them. After putting cream on them, she would tell them what good feet they were. She thanked them for carrying her everywhere and for the great job they did. I never forgot that. That kind of 'body appreciation' stuck in my mind. It was not body appreciation alone, but also an engagement of the soul as she showed appreciation, thankfulness and gratitude for a part of herself that is so often neglected, forgotten and taken for granted. It was a way of loving herself.

Speak to Your Brain

In trauma, we need to love ourselves and learn to reconnect and engage body and soul. I realised this when I thought about the brain and how neglected it is. People of faith will pray for healing of almost any part of the body, but in 30 years I had never heard anyone pray for healing for someone's brain. We put our hands on hurting parts of our body as a natural response, but do we ever consciously put our hands on our head to bring healing touch to our brain when it experiences trauma? How often do we speak to our brains with words of affirmation and appreciation?

I began doing this and was surprised at how healing it felt. I sat in a comfy, quiet place for a few minutes, took deeper, slower breaths to relax myself, put my hands on my head and began speaking to my brain. I said words like these:

> 'Brain, you have been through a terrible experience and I know how difficult it has been, and still is. But I want to thank you for working so hard, for trying to find a way through this. You are doing such an amazing job. I want you to know that we may not have all the answers to this situation, but you can rest, you can be at peace. Amygdala (the emotional part of my brain that stores memories), you do not need to overwork. I tell you to be calm, be at peace. Pre-frontal cortex (the reasoning, decision-making, logical part of the brain that goes to 'sleep' when traumatised), I tell you that your judgement and decision-making abilities are good.

The neural pathways in my brain are healing. I love you. I appreciate you.'

That might sound really odd to you! However, I urge you to try it. You certainly cannot lose anything from doing so, and you might actually discover a form of self-therapy that you can take anywhere, use at almost any time, and doesn't cost you a penny.

Healing Hands

There is something very special and therapeutic about touch from a human hand. It can be very healing. Hugs involve hands. We use hands to comfort and reassure others, we hold hands to express love. We use hands to gesticulate and express ourselves as we talk. Hands are powerful channels of our thoughts and emotions. We can use them to transmit peace, healing, and calm to others.

The therapies I have mentioned involve hands in some way. Prayer for healing often involves the laying on of hands too. A significant other in our lives can help by using their hands to bring a healing touch through massage, calm presence and reassurance, gentle stroking and hugging. But there will be times when you are alone, or when no-one else can help. At those times, you can help yourself.

You can put on some healing music, just be quiet in the stillness, or speak gently to yourself. Use your own hands to help your own body and soul re-engage with each other through a sense of touch.

- Put the palms of your hands on your head and gently and slowly stroke your hands down your hair, acknowledging and appreciating the shape of your skull, the life of your brain, the sensation of hair on your hands. Thank your head.

- Bring your hands down to your ears and feel the curves and shapes and the softness of the lobes. Thank your ears.

- Now, put the palms of your hands on your face and gently stroke outwards, feeling the sensation on your skin, the bone structure, eyebrows, cheekbones, acknowledging yourself and your uniqueness. Thank your face.

- Move your hands to the back of your neck, bring them forward, stroking your neck and then move them slowly onto your shoulders, smoothing away tension, breathing out stress. Thank your neck and shoulders.

- Using your right hand, slowly stroke your left arm from the top to the bottom, up and down as many times as you want. Use your left hand to do the same to your right arm. Thank your arms.

- Use your hands to love each other. Use one hand to stroke the back of the other and then reverse. Clasp them gently, stroke between your fingers, look at the back and front of your hands as you stroke them. Thank your hands for the work they do.

- Move your hands down to your chest and torso. Put your hand on your heart, put both hands on your heart. Close your eyes. Feel it beating. Take a deep breath and thank your heart.

- Put your hand on your stomach. Gently and slowly stroke it in circular motions clockwise or side to side. Breathe deeply. Stay still and calm and relaxed as you gently stroke and appreciate it. Thank your stomach.

- Move to your abdomen and pelvis. Move your hands gently around those areas and around your hips, buttocks and inner thighs. If you have suffered traumatic childbirth, miscarriage, or sexual abuse, this is a good time to love and appreciate these areas of your body. If you have a child that has caused you hurt or harm, or suffered the loss of a child, these are key areas that helped bring that child into the world, and that can harbour the stress of trauma. Stroke them gently and slowly and speak words of love, healing and appreciation to them.

- Move down to your thighs and lower leg, touching, stroking and appreciating. If you have injuries or scars, run a hand gently over them with love. Thank your legs.

- Finally, move to your feet. Sit down for this, or for any part of this process. Love your feet with your hands, along the top and the sole, between the toes, gently stroking, massaging. Thank your feet.

Movement

Movement is a powerful form of expression, relieves stress, increases serotonin, and connects body and soul.

Put on some music that you love and 'dance' to it. The movements can be more extreme, barely perceptible or anywhere in between. The secret is to move to the music in any way you want. You can do this when no-one is around so that you feel truly free. Experiment with movements such as flexing the hands and fingers, stretching them wide, rotating the hands at the wrist with the arms stretched out. Feel the use of the muscles. Reach to the side and in front as far as you can, as if reaching for an object. Tilt your head back as if you were looking at the sky and open your mouth as wide as it will go, stretching out the jaw and face muscles. Feel the sensation. Express yourself in any way you want to, enjoying the sensations of the movements.

Any form of movement and exercise can be helpful in releasing serotonin in the body and making you feel better. You can exercise to a video if preferred. The activity above, however, gives you a chance to put yourself into the movement. You can use the healing hands self-touch I mentioned earlier at the same time as the movement too.

Engaging with and getting in touch with our bodies through movement and touch is a huge stress reliever which can really make the difference each day when dealing with trauma.

8. Helping Others

This may not be a good time yet for you to even consider helping others. The sheer exhaustion of dealing with trauma and PTSD can leave you feeling that you have nothing to give and no energy to give it. However, you would be surprised just how much you have to give others. There are few people who understand how to communicate or empathise with those going through trauma. Having experienced it yourself, you will have the growing ability to do so. Because of what you have been through, or are going through, you will have an empathy others don't possess. You won't make some of the glib remarks people make or place expectations on people. You won't judge or condemn. You won't expect others to 'just get over it'. You have become an invaluable asset in the lives of others in this world.

You may not feel like helping others. You may even feel resentful of the suggestion. After all, why should you help others when you have been subjected to so much damage and suffering yourself? I do understand that feeling from my own experience. However, being able to input into the lives of suffering and traumatised people will benefit you too.

You will discover just how much you have come to learn and understand about trauma. You will discover how much you have grown in empathy and compassion. Helping others will get your mind off yourself and the pain and problem. It is a constructive distraction that gives a sense of purpose and a boost to confidence and self-esteem.

Helping others doesn't need to be a burden. You don't need that extra pressure. But it can be a natural outworking and outflow from your own experience of trauma. Your words of comfort will sound different to those who have never 'been there'. Your quiet presence and touch, even without words, could be the help someone needs at a critical time. The experience you have, the knowledge and understanding you have gained, and the tools you have learned about from this book, could even make the difference between life and death for someone.

Some of the best websites on trauma have not been written by doctors and professionals. They have been written by people like you, those who have experienced trauma and C/PTSD themselves.[51] These people have turned their trauma into something constructive to help other people. They have found purpose in their pain.

It is helpful to think that even in the midst of your pain there are opportunities for you to help others, maybe even save a suffering soul, help them on their journey, and give them purpose to their life too.

THE

SPIRITUAL

STEPS

Chapter 5

Spiritual Steps to Survive the Journey towards Healing

Not everyone has a faith or spiritual interest, but everyone can experience trauma. And everyone, no matter who they are or what they believe, is valuable and precious, and deserves all the help they can get in overcoming trauma. Spirituality can help.

If you are an atheist or agnostic, you may not believe in a spiritual world, or you may have your own interpretation of what the word 'spiritual' means. If you have no interest in spiritual things, or you equate spirituality solely with religion, you may think this chapter is not for you. But you would be wrong.

In this chapter, I speak from my own faith as a believer in Jesus Christ, a Christian. If you have no 'faith', you may feel that reading this chapter is unnecessary and want to skip it. Naturally there will be things here that you don't understand or make no sense to you. However, I do urge you to read as much as you can as there are useful principles here. If you read only one section, be sure to read the one on *forgiveness*. There, I relieve the *pressure* on traumatised people to forgive and give them *control* over forgiveness. And be sure to read Chapter 6 on Helping Others in Trauma and with PTSD, where you learn the important practicalities about what to do and what not to do!

But What Is Spirituality?

Firstly, let's take a look at what spirituality is.

The Oxford dictionary refers to spirituality as, 'the quality of being concerned with religion or the human spirit.' This definition is quite narrow and doesn't really tell us what the *human spirit* is so it is hard to understand from this what *spiritual* is.

The Collins Dictionary describes spirituality as, 'the state or quality of being dedicated to God, religion, or spiritual things or values, especially as contrasted with material or temporal ones.' This is a good definition. The body is a material thing so we know we are not talking about the body when using the word *spiritual*. We are talking about something other than material or temporary things of this world.

It can help to understand what spirituality means when we look at the words spirit and soul. There is some confusion about the words *spirit* and *soul*. What is the difference? The most useful and helpful way I have ever heard it described is like this:

> You *are* a spirit
> You *have* a soul
> You *live* in a body

You are a whole person with physical, mental, emotional, and spiritual needs.

The body is your *earth suit*. It gives you the permission and the ability to live on this earth. Whatever you believe about life after death, once your earth suit dies, you can no longer live here.

Your soul is your mind, will and emotions. These are vital parts of you that make up who you are, your personality, the way you think, what you feel and how you function personally.

Your spirit is you. It is the part of you that asks questions like:

Where did I come from?

Why was I born?

Why am I here?

What is my purpose?

Is there something else?

How did this earth come into being?

Is there a Some-one bigger than me?

Your spirit is the part that senses an emptiness which your soul and body try to fill with everything they can find, even if it is negative or bad for you, but it doesn't work. It is a void which cannot be filled with material or temporal things because it is a spiritual void. It can only be filled with spiritual answers to life.

Various spiritual beliefs employ all kinds of methods to connect with something bigger than themselves, to cope with the trials and traumas of life, to take charge of thoughts and feelings and have *authority* over them, and overcome self-limiting beliefs. From mindfulness to mantras, Shamanism and Buddhism, surrendering to *the Universe*,[52] and *The Law of Attraction*,[53] people are seeking ways to understand life, deal with life's challenges, and overcome their own limitations.

Spirituality is a normal part of life for the human. There is something of an overflow and interconnectedness between the spiritual and practical steps to dealing with trauma. They are not mutually exclusive. That is healthy. Our spiritual life impacts our practical life, and our practical life impacts our spiritual life.

That's why I have written a chapter on spiritual steps to help you survive and heal. This book is not in any way an attempt to discuss all forms of spirituality and beliefs. But while all other attempts at surviving trauma are good, the spiritual side of life can be very important in seeing us through. My faith has been both attacked by the trauma I have experienced, and been a vital part of seeing me through the trauma and helping me hold on to life. I am a Christian.54 That means I believe in Jesus and His crucifixion and resurrection, and in God as the one who created me and this Earth. Knowing Him has saved my life, changed my life, and given meaning and purpose to all I have been through. So, as I share the spiritual steps to surviving trauma, crisis & grief, I do so from the place of Christian spirituality.

The Effects of Trauma on Faith

Whatever our faith, and even with faith, trauma can upset all areas of our life, including the spiritual and practical aspects. Faith does not make a person immune to trauma. Trauma, especially when there is an overload of it, can upset our entire world, our thinking, our beliefs, our feelings of stability and security. It is like the boat of your life is suddenly on a vast ocean in a storm, waves going up and down, with no land in sight, making you sick. You want to get off but you can't.

When trauma affects our faith, it can get very scary. Some people don't seem to have a problem with their faith or with God when tragedy happens and trauma strikes. They hold on to their faith better. There could be many reasons for this, including how much trauma they have had in their past, and how much disappointment or disillusionment they have had in their life already. For some people, however, trauma turns their faith upside-down and inside-out. The effects of the trauma are frightening enough, but when it feels like we are losing our faith because of it, that can add a whole new level to the trauma.

When this happens, people need someone to blame. God is the obvious target. After all, He is the one who makes promises of protection, defence and care. So what happens when that doesn't seem to happen?

Blaming God is Normal

If you are blaming God for the trauma you have experienced, that is normal. Questions like: 'Why did He allow this to happen?', 'Why didn't He step in and do something?', 'Why didn't He stop it?', 'Are you even there?' are normal. It is even normal to question His love, care and protection. For some people, personal traumas and their view of the traumas in our world cause them to refute the existence of God. Trauma can bring doubts about all these things. Asking God these questions, being angry, shouting at God are all normal responses. You may feel like you don't want to be around spiritual things. You may not be able to pray or focus on things to do with God. You may find your trust in Him is damaged. This feels awful, but it is also normal. However, in the long run, none of this is going to help you survive on a journey towards healing. Why? Because while this thinking is normal and understandable, none of it is accurate. All of these responses are based in inaccurate beliefs about God. These simply push you further from the One who can bring help and healing.

Learning to separate God from a traumatic event is important. When I say *separate*, I don't mean that He wasn't there, that He was separated from you when it happened, off doing something else of greater divine importance! No. He sees and knows everything and never leaves or forsakes us. But we must learn to separate responsibility. In other words, God is not responsible for everything that happens. Some people attribute absolutely everything that happens to God, but this is *over-spiritual*.

Bad things happen but it doesn't mean God was responsible. And it doesn't mean He isn't grieved and angry about what happened too. God doesn't micromanage our lives and every single thing that happens. Some things just happen because we live in a fallen world tainted by the original sin of Adam and Eve, and which is full of human beings who can be selfish, irresponsible, thoughtless, dangerous and unkind, abusive and controlling.

Spiritual Abuse

Before we go any further, let's just talk a little about spiritual abuse. I mentioned this in Chapter 1.

Spiritual abuse occurs when people use God or another spiritual 'entity' to control you and your life in negative and extreme ways, get you to do something wrong, or do something wrong to you. We are all familiar with the concept of abuse, which can happen physically, emotionally, and sexually.

All the same feelings that come with trauma can happen with spiritual abuse in the same way as any other form of trauma, only it can be harder when you think God is somehow behind it, endorsing the behaviour, or in any way connected to it. He is not. Some ways of thinking that need to be remembered often by a person traumatised through spiritual abuse are:

- God is not happy with control and abuse in the Church, nor is He happy with those who do wrong to others and bring trauma into their lives;
- God feels grief, anger, and huge compassion towards those who are suffering from any kind of trauma;
- God cannot always correct wrongdoing or correct a situation immediately, however much we would like Him to. However, that does not mean it will not happen. As a Buddhist friend said to me on hearing of my own trauma, 'In my experience, when people do bad things to others, it has a way of coming back on them.' Buddhist or not, there is much truth in this principle. In a traumatised state it can be hard to see that God is at work for you or at work at all, but He is. Don't keep company with people who engage in spiritual abuse. Make sure you spend time with other sensitive believers or people of faith who are good for you, and in whom you can experience the true heart of a loving God towards you.

Never be afraid to recognise spiritual abuse for what it is, and to stand up to it. Never let it silence you.

Trauma from spiritual abuse can be particularly complex simply because there is a 'divine' element used. But we must remember God is not involved in any form of abuse, manipulation, coercion, or control. God must be separated from the event. He is *for* the traumatised and desires to correct controlling situations. However, damage is often already done to people before that happens. The feelings you have because of that damage are normal.

Always remember that you do not need to remain in a spiritually abusive or traumatising situation out of guilt, commitment, loyalty, or under threat. That is not God and it is not how He operates. He very much wants to reach into those areas of spiritual trauma, bring healing, and show you the truth about the loving, gracious God that He really is.

Normal!

You need to know that any of the feelings you have in response to any kind of trauma and grief are normal, and the negative effects on your faith are normal too! You may not feel normal. You may feel as far removed from your normal and from your faith that you have ever been. You may not feel normal in comparison with other people. You may not remember what 'normal' feels like. The whole of life might feel surreal right now. But all of those feelings are normal too. It is important your feelings are validated.

He is Not Your Enemy

It is also important to understand that God is not, never was, and never will be your enemy. Let me say that again. God is *not* your enemy. It may feel like He is. It may feel like He *allowed* something bad to happen to you when you believed He was good. It may feel like He doesn't love you or care for you, and that He is not good after all. That's how I felt after what happened to our family. But He is not the trouble maker. The Bible makes it clear that God's Son, Jesus, has come to give us life to the full and that we have an enemy, known as the *devil,* who comes to steal, kill and destroy.[55] God is light, and in Him is no darkness at all.[56] He goes around, as Jesus demonstrated, doing good and healing all who are oppressed by the devil.[57] He doesn't go about doing horrid things. There are plenty of people to do that. The Bible makes it clear that we live in a fallen, sin-infested world where bad things do happen and nasty people do nasty things. It makes it clear that there is an oppressive spirit or force behind this and darkness called the devil. In the midst of all that, Jesus came to save us from the self-destruction of sin and oppression, that we might have life, and that those who believe in Him would see and know the goodness of God as their Father. No matter what negative experience we have had, He is our healer, defender and protector, the answer to our prayers, the One who upholds us with His strength, and who can fill us with supernatural peace, even in turmoil.

But what happens when we don't feel protected, defended, upheld, or at peace? Sometimes, things do happen in this fallen world that cross all our boundaries of safety and peace. It's not fair. It's not the deal we wanted. It's not what we bought into. We want to stop the train and get off. We want our money back! What can we do?

1. Believe

It is right in the middle of this that what we believe is truly tested. This is the time when it is more important than ever, but more difficult than ever, to believe that God is who He says He is.

This is not easy at all. When faith goes through the fire of trauma, it can be terrifying. The degree of difficulty may depend on how much trauma you have been through previously in your life, and the nature of the recent trauma. It may depend on the area of your life it affects, and all that means to you. It won't always depend on the depth of your faith. It may, but there are times when no matter how strong you are spiritually, if something bad enough happens to even the strongest people of faith, they can begin to question and doubt.

After the amount of trauma I had suffered growing up, the trauma that affected my own family and motherhood was the 'straw that broke the camel's back' for me for many reasons. I don't think anyone would have ever believed that my faith would be affected. I certainly didn't. I was fully committed to Jesus from the time I first believed. Coming to know Him had saved my life and changed it completely for the better. Such was my gratitude and knowledge of His love for me, it seemed to be a faith beyond shaking in spite of all I had been through. I had hung on to that faith in many incredibly challenging circumstances for years. I was shocked and grieved when trauma seemed to steal my faith from me – I couldn't seem to stop it sliding from under my feet. The experience felt bitter and I was angry and resentful towards God. I could not carry on with the Christian work we had been doing for so many years in the same way. I had no more spiritual energy for it. I felt He had let me down, that I had been betrayed, that He had not kept His promises, that He had not kept His Word, and that believing and praying for years had been a waste of time.

The truth is that those feelings are normal. When terrible things happen, trust can be affected. It is just a reality of life in the darkest moments.

In the Bible, Joseph suffered terrible trauma (referred to in Chapter 3). Sometimes, I wonder what he must have thought as he languished in prison, fighting to bring purpose into that place and into his own future, unsure if he would ever get out. He had an advantage. He was young. He had youthful hope. As we get older, we have had more time to see and experience more things. We may have suffered more disappointments, disillusionment, betrayal, setbacks and unfulfilled dreams, and if a trauma hits us, it can knock us off our feet as we realise we have less time in life to make things work. God, the One we trust, can become the target for our anger. This can happen at any age, but as we get older it can hit harder if disappointments have built up over years or if life has not turned out the way we expected.

In the biblical account of Ruth and Naomi (also referred to in Chapter 3) we see how much trauma Naomi encountered. Naomi had seen a lot. She had seen her home town in the grip of famine, but had left with a new husband and hope to go to a new land and start again. She had every reason to believe in a bright and rosy future for her family. Then she was unexpectedly struck with the tragedy of both her sons being born with a disease that gradually killed them. Her husband died also. She was left with nothing but to return to her homeland and start again. Her confusion, anger, and disappointment were overwhelming and bitterness got the better of her. She still believed in God. She just didn't believe that He loved or cared for her like she did before. Through Boaz, her new son-in-law, God was able to show her that He did. In Naomi's case, moving to another place where she already had some family was the fresh start she needed. She needed to see some practical, real life evidences of God's goodness through people to regain trust and a sense of worth and value. It is especially important in times of trauma that we experience God with skin on! It is normal in trauma to have these needs.

Things don't always turn out as expected. Negative feelings are not surprising sometimes in the turmoil of life. God doesn't condemn us for struggling with extreme emotion when traumatic events take place. He knows the effect those kinds of things can have on our brains. Just like a bad fall can break a bone, trauma can change the pathways your brain normally uses to function well. It doesn't surprise Him. We don't need to condemn ourselves or feel guilty.

Believe He Is

What God asks is that we continue to believe two things about Him. Hebrews 11:6 tells us what those two things are:

> 'But without faith it is impossible to please Him,
> for he who comes to God must believe that **He is**,
> and that **He is a rewarder** of those who
> diligently seek Him.'

It doesn't say you can't feel angry or upset. It doesn't say you won't feel like your trust is impaired. It doesn't say your emotions will always be on an even keel. You may struggle with believing. You may fight, question, doubt, and believe again all in the space of one day and go through it all again the next day. What God asks us to do is *believe He is*. But what if you are shouting at Him and angry? If you are shouting at God that is good! Talking to Him, even shouting at Him in your confusion and fear from the trauma means you are still believing in Him, believing that *He is*, and still communicating. The trauma has simply caused you to doubt some of His characteristics. But it is those very characteristics that will help see you through. If you are tempted to stop believing in His existence, remember that neither your disbelief, nor the trauma you have experienced stop God existing. He still *is*. He may not *feel* present in the turmoil you are experiencing but He still is. God just *Is*.

Believe He Is a Rewarder

Right now, it might feel impossible to believe in His goodness, or that He is a *rewarder* for the times you have believed in Him and sought Him so diligently, year after year, month after month, day after day. There is nothing about the trauma that feels like anything close to a reward. It feels like completely the opposite. It feels like God has lied to you and instead of a reward, allowed you to suffer something terrible. Surely, Joseph and Naomi must have struggled with these thoughts and feelings, as did many others in the Bible.

During my time of trauma I still believed that He is. I sometimes doubted, but I knew non-belief was futile, simply separating me from the One who was most able to help. But I did have a hard time believing He is a rewarder.

When it feels hard to believe that God is good, that He has something good planned for us, we can feel like Jairus, a man in the Bible whose sick daughter was dying.[58] In anguish he sent a message to Jesus to ask Him to come and make her well. As Jesus was on the way to Jairus' house, Jairus was told that his daughter had just died. It was too late. Things couldn't get any worse. But Jesus said on His arrival to him,

'Don't be afraid. Only believe.'

The man, aware of his own inability to believe in such a traumatic situation yet desperate to do something, cried out,

'Lord, I believe! Help my unbelief!'[59]

We can hear his desperation, his awareness of his own doubts and weaknesses, his difficulty believing in God's ability to do anything in the crisis. But in that cry, we also hear his desperate desire to believe, his humble need for help.

And in Jairus, we can hear ourselves too. We recognise our own weakness to believe in the face of overwhelming trauma and fear. We too can cry out in the midst of the pain, shock and grief of trauma,

'I want to believe in your goodness but I cannot see it in the midst of this pain. Please help me see it. Help me believe. Please help my unbelief!' God likes that prayer. I believe that rather than seeing this as weak in faith, He sees that as a wonderful prayer. He sees humble strength in it. And it will be answered.

Another woman in the Bible who had to find belief in the midst of massive pain and disappointment was a woman who had been very ill for eighteen years. For all that time, she had an 'issue' of blood. Losing blood made her unclean and unacceptable in the culture and society at that time. She became an outcast. Aside from the fear, rejection, loneliness, and failing hope, just the practicalities alone were incredibly difficult as she tried to contain the problem. The blood loss meant daily weakness and lack of energy, and quite possibly anaemia and other health-related issues. It meant constantly trying to find practical ways to keep clean, the embarrassment of stained clothing, and the perpetual need for items to catch the flow. Imagine menstruating for eighteen years continuously!

On top of that, she had spent every penny she had on doctors to try and cure the problem and nothing had worked. She had lost her livelihood along with her health and was considered a social outcast for eighteen long, lonely, painful, miserable, uncomfortable, humiliating years.

Then Jesus came along. There was really no reason for her to believe that anything would work. She had tried it all. She could have been done with God and done with any kind of faith, trust or believing, and lived the rest of her life with the blood and bitterness. But in the midst of the pain, she determined to still believe, and chose the right place to put her faith and trust. In earnestness, faith, and desperation, she pushed through the crowd, telling herself over and over again that if she could just touch Jesus' clothes, she would be healed. She was 'unclean' and should not have gone anywhere near Him, but she broke the rules and did it anyway. She pushed through the crowd jostling around her, and reached out a hand towards His clothing. It happened just as she believed.[60] She was healed. There is something about that kind of pain that can either produce great bitterness, or produce great belief that God is able to do something good. I wonder whether we will allow our own pain to produce great bitterness or great belief?

Many of the Psalms show this paradox; this place where great trial and trauma can be found in the same place as great faith. The writers of the Psalms are not ashamed to admit the depth of the trial and trauma they are facing. They have trouble and enemies, those trying to destroy them, those who have forsaken them, betrayed and abandoned them, even in their own families. They have people lying about them and making violent threats. They are concerned with feeling forgotten by God, being abandoned by Him like they have been abandoned by people in their lives. But they are not afraid to cry out to God for deliverance and help. To do that however, they had to believe that God is and that He would in some way bring good to them. We often tend to interpret their cries as spiritually robust in the face of trouble, so faith-filled, so strong. But have we ever imagined these cries may have come through bitter tears, been spoken out in the midst of anguish, doubt and fear, through clenched teeth, the cries of the weak and desperately needy?

In the following Psalm, we see the writer struggling with what seems to be abandonment by his mother and father, and the actions of liars, and violent and cruel abuse.

> *'Hide not Your face from me; turn not Your servant away in anger, You who have been my help! Cast me not off, neither forsake me, O God of my salvation! Although my father and my mother have forsaken me, yet the Lord will take me up, adopt me as His child.* Teach me Your way, O Lord, and lead me in a plain and even path because of my enemies. *Give me not up to the will of my adversaries, for false witnesses have risen up against me; they breathe out cruelty and violence. What would have become of me had I not believed that I would see the Lord's goodness in the land of the living!* Wait, hope for and expect the Lord; be brave and of good courage and let your heart be stout and enduring. Yes, wait for and hope for and expect the Lord.'[61]

In the midst of the pain and trauma of abandonment, the danger and threats of enemies, and the fear that God will also abandon him, the psalmist continues to believe that he would somehow see *the goodness of the Lord* in his life. God is the one 'person' he *can* trust. His words exhort us, the readers, to believe, to hope, to expect God to do something. He doesn't say believing will always be easy. He tells us to be brave and courageous and that our hearts will need to be strong while we *wait, hope for, and expect* the Lord to do something.

Often in trauma we don't feel brave and courageous at all. But you don't have to feel brave or do courageous acts. In trauma, just staying alive is brave, and getting up to face another day is courageous. Just believing itself is an act of courage.

In the midst of trauma and all we are suffering, He doesn't expect us to do things alone. We can ask the Lord to help us to believe in His goodness; to help us believe that He will somehow be our help, comfort, strength, strong tower, mighty fortress, deliverer, restorer, healer and redeemer.

I wish that when we cry out to God in this way, things always happen immediately. When we are suffering the challenges of trauma, we need instant help! It can feel strange to cry out to God and not get instant and immediate help from the one we call our Father, especially when we are in pain. We need Him to instantly reverse the situation and remove the pain. If we don't get instant help, it can make us think that He doesn't care. However, that is not true. He cares very, very much. Sometimes, we may receive instant help in the form of an encouragement from a friend, a still small voice that He speaks to us, some happy news, a supportive spouse, constructive help, or some new thing we learn to help us through another day on a journey moving forward to a better place. Often, we don't notice these things as God's support and help, seeing us through, bit by bit, day by day. Trauma is an earth-shattering, negative event for a person. We often feel like we need corresponding earth-shattering positive events to make up for the negative ones and make us feel better. But the positives often come in the form of small things that happen, one here, and one there. The traumatised mind often misses those small events because they don't impress themselves on our minds enough. But you will start to notice them again. Better things will come. It is not possible to say how long it will take. But your ability to see the positives and see the good things God is bringing into your life will be restored.

I struggled for over three years, the traumatic event still going on, wondering if God would ever 'show up', trying to appreciate the small, good things that happened, but finding them an inadequate compensation for the trauma I was suffering. And then, suddenly, some things started to happen that were more meaningful and special, things I had wanted to do for many years but had never worked out. The trauma hadn't stopped but something good began again in my life. And it will in yours. He is not a magician. He will not wave a wand and suddenly everything is better. I wish it was that way! But the God who sees everything at the same time, will order events to bring good into your life. It may take some time. But He will support you on the journey.

He knows our broken hearts and how difficult it can be sometimes to believe with a broken heart. He is acquainted with grief Himself. He would have lived His life knowing He was marked for something different, destined for death, God in flesh grieving at the depravity of humanity and the pain and suffering He witnessed. He was awaiting the day when He would have to say goodbye to His friends and loved ones, watching His mother weep as He hung on the cross in the agony of the cross itself, but also the agony of the betrayal, lies and treachery He experienced. And yet He did it for us. He understands grief. He wants to help bear the burden of the sorrows and grief we feel and carry it for us. God sent Jesus to heal the broken-hearted. He can heal your heart. He can heal your mind. He can heal your brain from trauma. He can heal PTSD.

It is also important to believe that you *can* heal. It is important to believe that PTSD does not have the last say, that you do not have to endure this for the rest of your life. It is important to believe that the effects of trauma can be healed and that you can go on to something better. It was a defining moment for me when I chose to believe these things. You may find it hard to believe those things right now, but belief is one of the things that is under your control. Ask God to help you make that switch from believing everything negative, to believing something positively. It really does make a difference to how your brain functions and repairs, and to your life. Believing brings fresh hope.

He can restore your soul. He can redeem your situation. He can redeem mine. It may not all look like it did before. But like Joseph and Naomi, He can bring good things, and a new beginning.

> 'Surely He has borne our griefs and carried our sorrows and pains. He was a man of sorrows and acquainted with grief. He heals the broken hearted and binds up their wounds.'[62]

Somehow, this is possible.

2. Take Authority Over Your Mind

Taking authority over your mind is an important spiritual step. What does that mean? Really it means you having the *control* over your mind. We talked about the importance of words and thoughts earlier in the book, but now we will look at it in a spiritual light.

People adopt various strategies in order to take charge of their thoughts and feelings, such as mindfulness, speaking mantras, and surrendering and/or praying to 'the universe'. Christians, however, draw on a power beyond themselves and a relationship with a loving Father. They pray to God and use the name of Jesus in their prayers. The name of Jesus is powerful, not because there is anything special in that name alone, but because of who Jesus is, what He has done, and because when the believer speaks His name with authority and faith, it has great power. The Bible tells us that Jesus is 'the name above all names' and that believers can *ask* anything in His name.[63] A literal translation for the word *'ask'* here is *demand*. God also tells us that He has given us *all authority* over the enemy.[64] So we can use the name of Jesus to ask or demand with authority.

The trauma itself, the injury from it, the grief and depression, the PTSD, the intrusive thoughts, and every other possible negative result from the trauma can all be initiated and utilised by the enemy of our souls to destroy us, our belief in God and our relationship with Him. However, we don't have to be subject to that. We can speak to ourselves and our minds in His name.

Speak to Your Mind

By speaking to our mind, we can learn to regain control and authority over it. We need to use the authority we have been given in Christ, and in the name of Jesus, to take authority over depression, and over intrusive thoughts and images that keep returning to re-traumatise us. In trauma, these intrusive, repetitive thoughts that involuntarily replay events over and over again can be very hard to control. They can make you feel like you are going crazy. But you can say 'NO' to them. You can put your hand on your head and say,

'In Jesus' name, I tell these intrusive thoughts and images to leave my mind and leave me alone.'

You can speak in that way as often as you need to. You were created by God. Your mind belongs to Christ. One day, this sentence came to my mind, and I sensed that God was telling me to say this phrase to myself,

'My mind is Christ's sacred place.'

My mind is not a place to allow the enemy to torment me. My mind is created by God and it is sacred. It belongs to Christ. It is the birthing and germinating place for ideas and creativity. It is His, the Creator's studio where His works of art are created. It is not a junk yard to allow the enemy to throw his trash. It's not a place to let the devil dance in. It is sacred. It is Christ's dancing place. It is His temple for holy use. Say the following to yourself out loud:

'My mind is Christ's sacred place. I have the mind of Christ and hold the thoughts, intents and purposes of His heart.'[65]

You will find your own words and phrases that have special meaning to you and you can ask God to give you specific words unique to you.

Think on Good Things

The Bible tells us to think on things that are good, noble, true, lovely, gracious and of good report.[66] There is always going to be something in our head, either positive or negative. Don't allow your mind to just do its own thing, spinning and free-wheeling on neutral. Put it into gear. Deliberately fill it with good thoughts to replace the negative ones with good memories, positive experiences, healthy music, and encouraging words. This takes more work to do when you have experienced trauma, but it will help you to survive.

When your mind is filled with fear and confusion, you can imagine you are in the boat with Jesus. Jesus was sailing over the sea with his disciples and fell asleep in the boat. A fierce storm came up and the disciples, some of whom were rugged fishermen, were afraid. That shows how fierce the storm must have been. But Jesus was asleep in the boat, at peace and unafraid. Sometimes, when I am afraid and feel unsafe and insecure, I picture that scene. In my mind, I imagine that I am lying down in that boat with Jesus. The storm may be howling around me, the boat going up and down on the huge waves, but I am lying safely curled up with Jesus, asleep and at peace. That is a useful exercise for the mind to help you to relax and deal with anxious thoughts.

Your mind belongs to God. Your brain was created by Him as the hub of your body and soul. He cares about it. People often pray for healing from various sicknesses.

You can also lay your hand on your head and pray healing over your brain. You could pray something like this:

> *'Thank you, Lord, that you are the healer. In your name, I speak healing to my brain. I take authority over the negative effects of trauma in the name of Jesus. I command those damaged pathways to be healed and restored. I command my brain to be healthy and function well.'*

You can pray whatever you feel is helpful to you and as God leads according to your own circumstances.

Taking back control of your mind is a process. With prayers like the one you just read, speaking to your mind, and with God's help, you can make strides in regaining control from the trauma-induced negative images. However, be patient. It can also be a process that takes time. Don't be disappointed if the process is slow. That is normal. What is marvellous is that you can engage in that process with God, and you and He can travel that road together.

3. Be Thankful

I mentioned words to use in thankfulness earlier in the practical steps. But thankfulness is also a very spiritual exercise. When the problem, injustice, crisis, grief, loss and trauma are so big in your life and in your mind, it can stop you from thinking about anything else. It gets hard to see the good things in your life. I remember a woman preacher saying that if you have one child giving you hell, thank God for the two that aren't. It is a helpful principle. If you have lost, thank God for what you haven't lost. If you are grieving from death, see if you can find a small light of thankfulness for what lives. If something is wrong, be thankful for what is right. If there is something you can't do, thank God for what you can do.

Being thankful is not always easy. Sometimes we are hurting too much to feel thankful or even say something that sounds thankful or grateful. Anger is normal in trauma and it can be difficult to feel angry and thankful at the same time. A disillusioned, disappointed heart can become a critical, sharp and negative tongue because of the pain. A depressed spirit can find thankfulness exhausting. It can take a real effort when you feel traumatised to be thankful. At times, you really feel that there is nothing to be thankful for because you are so crushed by the traumatic event/s you have been through. The trauma has overwhelmed and consumed everything. But if you look, there will be things for which to be thankful. They may seem like such small things that they are hidden in the darkness. If you can't find them now, look again in five minutes. Look again in an hour. Look again tomorrow. Look again in a week. Keep looking. There will come moments when you feel a bit better and you can again see some of the good things. As you start to vocalise some of the things to be thankful for, however small they seem, you help to change the pathways in your brain from their negative default position and help with the healing, construction and formation of new positive pathways.

Here is a list of simple things we sometimes take for granted and forget to be thankful for:

Your hands. Hold them up in front of you and look at them. Turn them over and move them about. They do wonderful things for you every day.
A roof over your head
A meal in front of you
Three meals a day
A warm, dry place to sleep
Water from a tap
Hot water
Utilities such as gas and electricity
Technology such as a computer or a phone
A car to drive
Your health
Your legs
The ability to read and write
Prescription eye glasses
A toilet
Family and friends
A church gathering
Clothes to wear.

This list could go on and on. You could make your own. The more you really think about things to be thankful for, the more the list keeps growing and the more thankful you feel. I decided to be thankful for three things every time we sat down for dinner. My husband helped me to remember to do it. It only took a minute of my day, but that little activity helped to make a difference in my thinking. Just one small, positive activity like that each day can help your brain.

Being thankful is an important form of praise. Praise silences the enemy.[67] The enemy of our souls is trying to silence you, to destroy you, but praise and thanksgiving silence *him*. He wants to shut you up with the trauma, but your thankfulness and praise shut him up. The Bible tells us that when you make a sacrifice of praise, it actually makes a way for God to show you His salvation.[68] When thankfulness towards God is difficult, remember that you are making a sacrifice by doing it. However, He sees the effort made in that sacrifice. It has great power. It makes a way for God to bring change and bring *salvation* into your life and your situation.

4. Forgive? (If you read one section in the Spiritual Steps chapter, read this one!)

I have put the subject of forgiveness in the chapter on Spiritual Steps because it is a deeply spiritual exercise. However, if you do not consider yourself a *spiritual* person or person of faith, read this anyway, because it is also a very practical issue. The subject of forgiveness is not an easy one and I don't talk about it lightly. If the concept of forgiveness makes you feel angry, read on through the first few paragraphs because you will see that in the latter part of this step, I do not pressurise anyone to forgive.

If the trauma you have been through involves abuse and betrayal, especially by those who should have loved you and whom you trusted, forgiveness can be particularly hard. Often it is not just the forgiving that is hard, but the fact that forgiveness is an expected action which can add a great burden to what you are already suffering. On top of that, even if you do forgive, you are still in pain. You might have heard from Christian sources the idea that if you have truly forgiven, you will no longer feel the pain of what was done to you.

Your forgiveness of those who wronged you might prevent bitterness from growing in your heart, but it does not necessarily take away the pain of what was done and the damage it caused to you and your life. If you are still in pain, you can feel guilty and end up having to practice forgiveness on a daily basis, only to discover that the pain remains. All this hard work of trying to forgive, the pain which seems to tell you that you haven't really forgiven, and the subsequent guilt, can be confusing and cause resentment. Then you are back to having to forgive again and asking forgiveness for yourself too! It can be a cycle that seems to go around and around. Now you are burdened with the injustice done to you, the forgiving to do, the pain making you feel like you haven't forgiven, and the guilt. All that, and you were not the one who did the wrong in the first place! That can feel like a terrible and cruel burden.

I believe Christ can enable forgiveness, but I also believe that Christians talk about forgiveness far too freely, usually the forgiveness that *others* have to do. That's easy for them when they are not the ones who have been through the trauma! Even if they have been through terrible trauma themselves, they are not *you*, and they have not experienced *your* trauma. Their ability to forgive may be an inspiration to you to help you forgive. If so, that is a wonderful and constructive thing. However, if their ability to forgive just makes you feel guilty, that is no help at all.

For a truly traumatised person, forgiveness takes time, effort, faith, energy, and a huge generosity of spirit that is hard to find in the midst of their own anguish. We should never demand it. We should never pressurise to get forgiveness from a person and never make them feel guilty or condemned. The idea of forgiveness can be gently raised and encouraged, but the timing of that must be very sensitive. Never, ever mention forgiveness to someone just after a traumatic event, the loss of a loved one, or abuse.

Forgiveness must come at their own volition, in their own time and own way, at their pace. It cannot always be done in one go (there may be exceptions but we should certainly not expect that). It may be the ongoing process of a lifetime in some cases and that is a weighty thing to carry. You have no right to try to get forgiveness out of someone who is not ready to do it themselves. You will only increase their distress and bring shame and blame upon them as a victim of trauma.

We do know, however, that God asks believers in Him to forgive. But is it actually quite that simple? Have we 'fundamentalised' scripture and turned it into a command that now causes further trauma for those already traumatised? According to the stories and accounts I have heard from others, it seems to be the case.

I go into more detail about forgiveness in my book, *Take Courage: Finding Courage in God to Live.* There are many good reasons to forgive that are beneficial and right. However, for the purposes of *this* book I would like to say that *the emphasis by others should never be on the victim having to forgive, but on the perpetrator being held to account.*

We must call things what they are. Wrong is wrong. Abuse is wrong. Evil is evil. Crime is crime. The law is the law. Abuse and crime should be addressed through the proper channels. Those who do wrong should be confronted. There should be accountability, responsibility, the encouragement of remorse, genuine apology, and the outworking of positive change and rebuilding of trust by the perpetrator. Victims of abuse and trauma should be kept safe from further harm.

The purpose of working through forgiveness is *not* to let the offender off scot-free. Any process of forgiveness is done *for our own sake and benefit,* and in response to how we individually hear God speak to us from His Word, or because of our own personal conviction to do so as we are able.

Asking a person to forgive the remorseless murderer of their child who then gets out of prison early is a tall order, and one we have no right to demand. Only the victim's family can decide how, when and if they might work through forgiveness. The victim of a rape who suffers PTSD, and a subsequent broken marriage and loss of employment, is the only one who can determine what forgiveness might mean in their life. It cannot be imposed from the outside.

Whether someone is of faith or not, those who choose forgiveness, or do it as an act of obedience to what they believe God says, need love, care and support. We should never think that because people have chosen to forgive they no longer feel pain, anger, bitterness, or that their lives have not been significantly damaged by the trauma. We should never believe that once someone has forgiven, everything is okay, and the ensuing pain and problems are all gone.

We should never tell people that if they forgive someone properly, they won't feel any more pain or hurt. A person who has been deeply traumatised through abuse, betrayal or abandonment often feels the pain, rejection and trauma long after forgiveness has taken place. Memories stored in the brain and body mean they have to live with the effects of trauma and find ways to survive and manage the symptoms on the journey towards healing, which is what this book is about. It is also why we must be so careful not to put negative things in the lives of others that could have a long-lasting negative impact on them. Traumatising others puts *them* in this same difficult situation of having to try to forgive. If only people were kind to one another as they should be, we wouldn't have this to deal with.

It does happen however. And when it does, forgiveness is for our own benefit, not for the benefit of the one who has caused damage. If there is long-term bitterness and anger associated with unforgiveness, the ongoing stress can cause accompanying sickness in the body. The purpose of forgiveness is to help prevent this. Forgiveness is *not* to help the person who did wrong. It is to help *you*.

You don't have to *feel* forgiving in order to forgive. In fact, it would be unrealistic and even cruel to expect a person to generate positive feelings towards a perpetrator of deep trauma. While this might be possible with the help of Christ in some cases, it is certainly not going to be the general rule. Nor is it a sign of lesser spirituality if a person does not have those feelings.

Forgiveness is done by faith, not feeling. You don't have to feel forgiving to do it. You can ask God to help you do it. As you say it with your mouth, you may not always feel it in your heart, but you do it anyway, by faith. If you want to and are ready to work through the process of forgiveness, it should not be a further traumatic burden for you. It can be done simply.

When you forgive, say the person's name. Here are some simple words you can use:

'I forgive.....by faith' and put their name in the space. You can also speak out what you forgive them for if you are able to.

You can write down the date you forgave if it helps. When feelings of pain or guilt come, or lies telling you that you haven't really forgiven, you can say, 'No. That's not true. I forgave them then, and I continue to forgive now.' You can do that as often as you want. There is nowhere that God says forgiveness has to be a one-time event.

Don't wait for all the right feelings to come in order to forgive. It could be a long wait. Once, after an abusive church situation, I forgave almost immediately through anguish and tears but remained in pain for months, and depressed for three years. The event impacted my life and the life of our family. I was able to recover better when we left the country to continue overseas work and leave all the places and people behind that triggered the memories of that event. When I felt more well myself, I was able to have greater *feelings* of forgiveness and think less and less about the situation. Seven years later, the perpetrator of the abuse contacted me to apologise for what they had done. While they had spent some of those years experiencing first-hand the abuse they had dished out to me, I was glad I had spent those seven years in a place of forgiveness rather than wasting energy and life on growing bitterness or resentment.

Many years later, our family was subjected to an abusive situation by a loved one in league with complete strangers. This event triggered PTSD symptoms in me and once again impacted our family, but this time in an even greater way. It was a year and a half after I forgave this betrayal that I even began to have real *feelings* of forgiveness, and those were not consistent or long lasting and were still interspersed with grief, pain and anger. There is nothing wrong with that. It's quite normal. Anger due to abuse and trauma is a normal, healthy response to wrong-doing. The purpose of forgiveness is not to deprive you of these natural, normal and right emotions. Three years later, and especially because the trauma was ongoing, there was still pain and anger. And that is okay. It didn't mean I had not forgiven them. I continued to speak out forgiveness, not for their benefit but for my own. It took a long time for God to work through the layers of pain caused by the trauma. I had forgiven by faith, not by feeling. I was in pain and traumatised so it was hard to feel anything good.

When you forgive by faith you do it because it is good for *you*, and will keep bitterness from taking permanent root, keep you from destructive hatred, and keep your heart soft. This is healthier for you, gives God a better opportunity to work in the situation, take any vengeance or make any changes necessary in the life of the person who did wrong, and do good things in your life.

Forgiving does not make the wrong someone did acceptable. It does not mean they should not be punished. It doesn't make what has happened okay. It does not mean you should not talk about what has happened. It simply helps release you from further destructive emotions that could grow and become harmful to you.

Forgive & Forget?

Some people say that forgiving means forgetting. However, a traumatised person must never be made to feel guilty for bringing up a wrong done to them. They must be allowed to talk about it. This is a very important part of grief and processing the event, and that processing can go on for a long time. They should not be expected or told to just forget about it.

In many cases, we can just forget the minor offenses of everyday life. However, there are some things we should not forget. For example, if someone has sexually abused us, is violent or dangerous, has betrayed trust, or has manipulated and coerced us into something wrong, we may forgive them, but we don't have to forget what they did or be around them again. We don't have to trust them or be their friend, or work with them. That is not unforgiveness. That is good sense, especially if there is a chance of the behaviour being repeated.

If you burn yourself on a stove, you don't put your hand back into it again. There is an old saying, 'Once bitten, twice shy.' It basically means that if you get bitten by something, you are more careful of it next time. If a dog bites you, you probably won't go near that dog again in order to protect yourself from the potential of further harm. We should not forget what is dangerous. That is an important boundary for everyone, but especially those suffering the effects of trauma. Some things you remember for your own safety and protection. You don't forget them. If someone has done you serious harm, they would certainly need to prove to you that they had genuinely changed and your trust would have to be regained on your terms, if you were to continue any kind of friendship or relationship with them. It may even be necessary to ensure that only happened in the presence of other people too. In fact, I would recommend it. You don't just forget the danger.

If you are afraid of people or situations unnecessarily, frightened of something that is no longer a danger or threat, or unable to trust in someone who is trustworthy, that is a result of the trauma and you could be having symptoms of PTSD. It is sensible to see a medical professional who may be able to diagnose you with PTSD.

Forgive as *you* are able, in *your* time. And exercise forgetfulness when you are able in situations where you know you are safe and trust is restored. You may need help in forgiving by talking it through and praying with a trusted person. However, make sure it is with people who let you go at your own pace and let *you* be ready, so all that you do and say in terms of forgiveness is genuine, sincere, and from your own heart. It may not be perfect, it may not *feel* great, but God knows and understands your readiness at each stage of forgiving. And if you can't forgive? Don't worry. Focus on what you *can* do to help yourself at this time.

Do We Need to Forgive At All?

There is a growing body of thought and articles saying that it is wrong to expect the severely abused, traumatised, and those suffering from PTSD and C-PTSD to forgive, or that forgiving is not necessary for healing. Some people do come to a place of healing without forgiving.

Having suffered myself I do understand the thinking on this. We have no right to demand forgiveness or pass judgement on victims who choose not to forgive. For some people, the concept of forgiving on top of the awful abuse they have suffered is more than they can bear and the only element of the situation over which they feel they have control. And we must ask ourselves this question: Just how easy is forgiveness for a person who has suffered years of abuse at the hands of their own relative, been held in captivity as a sex slave, and repeatedly traumatised? We absolutely must be sensitive to this.

For some, forgiveness carries the idea of letting the person off, and for them that is unthinkable. This is not true, of course, as the purpose of forgiveness is to benefit the forgiver, but it certainly can feel as if it is to benefit the offender. We must acknowledge how the concept of forgiveness makes people feel in any given situation.

Making the victim feel guilty for not forgiving is a pointless and destructive exercise. Compassion and understanding is needed. This is far more likely to help generate the possibility and ability to forgive than shame and blame. Shame and blame should *never* be put on the victim.

In the case of those who believe in Jesus, we are told to forgive. However, the expectation is not supposed to be all on the victim. We are also told to go to the offender (if they are in the church) and tell them their wrong. This gives them an opportunity for remorse and to apologise and ask for forgiveness. If they will not listen, we are told to go with someone else. And if they still will not listen, we are to take the issue to the church.[69] The church then has a responsibility to deal with the offender. If they do not, or they protect them, they cause further trauma for the person already traumatised. In going to the offender, the object is to help the person understand what they did in the hopes of remorse and *asking* for forgiveness. Remember, forgiving someone who shows remorse and who genuinely *asks* for forgiveness is going to be that much easier than forgiving someone who shows no remorse, couldn't care less about the damage they have done to you, and who would probably damage you further if they could.

The Church of England's guidance on forgiveness and reconciliation emphasizes the importance of offering sensitive care to those who have been abused and avoiding suggesting forgiveness is easy, instantaneous, or a condition of God loving an individual (Church House Publishing, 2017.)[70]

Whether inside or outside the church, we would do well to remember this.

What if you are not a believer, and have no church connections? You can use the same principles. You can ask a member of the family or friend to go with you to the person who has done harm. If it is in a company or business context, there may be a higher authority you could then go to. It may even be a situation, such as a crime or abuse, where that higher authority should be the police.

Whatever the situation, whether church-related or not, no-one should be afraid to go to the police where issues of abuse warrant action from a higher authority. People in churches should never submit to pressure to keep quiet about abuse or be hushed up to keep it in the boundaries of the church, and should never remain quiet where the law is being broken.

When going to others to seek resolution, there is no guarantee either in a church context or outside of it that you will elicit the apology required. It is at that point that you will be faced with a decision on how to proceed in a way that is best for you. You might find the help of a minister, a close friend, or supportive family can undergird you as you decide what to do.

Forgiveness is possible. Christ does enable us to forgive. However, I also know that Christian people suffer trauma like anyone else. Being a Christian does not make you immune to the effects of trauma. Demanding forgiveness is not appropriate. Whether we have faith or not, we must always remember forgiveness is for our own benefit, not the benefit of the wrongdoer. We must be allowed to do it in our own time, in our way, at our pace, with God's help, and never be bullied, pressurised, or shamed into it. Once again, forgiveness is done by faith, you don't have to feel forgiving, you don't have to forget, and it is under your control.

5. Do Something Different

Those suffering from the effects of grief and trauma, and experiencing C-PTSD do not want to go through what they are going through. They would give anything to go back, to prevent the trauma from ever having happened, to put the situation right, to wake up and find it was all just a dream (or nightmare), to just be able to remove the pain. Nobody wants to stay in the place of trauma. It is too uncomfortable.

You have a spiritual enemy, however, who wants to make it so familiar to you, like a bad 'friend', so that you stay in that traumatised place even though you don't want to. He wants to keep you stuck at a certain point so you don't find any new beginning. He wants to prevent you from moving forward at all and keep you from finding any kind of healing or better place in your life. Don't let him do that to you.

One time I sensed the Lord say to me,

'If you want to feel different and you want things to be different, you have to do something different.'

The same thought patterns, words, negativity, behaviour, activities, and actions can all serve to keep you in exactly the same place next year. If you want something different, you must do something different.

The enemy of your soul wants to keep you stuck at a certain point, unable to move, disabled and crippled. But God wants to help you through, help you move, give you strength, and take you forward to a new beginning. To do that, you need to cooperate with Him and do something different. He can't do it for you but He can help you.

Doing 'something different' is taking a step that goes beyond where you are now, however small it is. It's a form of spiritual warfare. It's not easy. I think engaging in spiritual warfare from a place of trauma is very tough. Who feels like fighting some unseen enemy when you are having a hard time finding the motivation to get dressed in the morning? How can soldiers already wounded on the battlefield fight an intense battle? Trauma *is* a battle. But you *can* do it. You may not look or feel like any kind of fighter or warrior. But you do have a warrior Spirit, the Holy Spirit, inside you. The fact that you are still alive and reading this book is proof of that! But you don't need to fight alone and God doesn't want you to. He wants to fight with you and for you through His people. Ask others to pray for you. Get a friend or relative to set up a support circle or group that can pray as often as they are able and agree together on your behalf, and pray for strength for you. He wants to be your greatest help but He will engage His people too to be a support, even if it is just a special friend, a couple or handful of people. He wants to engage every possible means of strengthening you and lifting you up.

In the following words we see the writer, David, explaining the help he has found in God in extremely challenging circumstances.

In Psalm 18 verses 4-6 we see the distress, anguish, and terror David is feeling. He feels hemmed in, face-to-face with death, face-to-face with hell itself.

> 'The cords or bands of death surrounded me, and
> the streams of ungodliness and the torrents of ruin
> terrified me. The cords of Sheol (the place of the
> dead) surrounded me; the snares of death
> confronted and came upon me. In my distress
> [when seemingly closed in] I called upon the Lord
> and cried to my God; He heard my voice out of His
> temple (heavenly dwelling place), and my cry

came before Him, into His [very] ears.'

In verses 28-35 we see how God wants to be in our lives in the darkest moments, how He wants to help us 'make progress on the dangerous heights of testing and trouble'.

> *'For You cause my lamp to be lighted and to shine; the Lord my God illumines my darkness. For by You I can run through a troop, and by my God I can leap over a wall...He is a shield to all those who take refuge and put their trust in Him...who girds me with strength...He makes my feet like hinds' feet [able to stand firmly or make progress on the **dangerous heights** of testing and trouble]; He sets me securely upon my high places. He teaches my hands to war, so that my arms can bend a bow of bronze. You have also given me the shield of Your salvation, and Your right hand has held me up...'[71]*

Dangerous heights? That is how it feels. Beyond us. Too much to cope with. But He knows. And He wants to help us make progress, to keep moving forward to a better place. He will help. But we need to work with Him and do what we can. To move from where we are, we need to do something different.

Your feelings tell you one thing. They talk about the pain, they remind you of the trauma you have been through, some of which may even be ongoing. Your feelings are completely valid. But to survive and move forward, you will need to tell your feelings something else. You will need to do something positive and different that your feelings keep telling you not to do. It might just be a small thing, but every small step is an achievement that makes a difference.

Let me give you an example. My greatest gift is communication. I naturally communicate in many ways, through speaking, writing, art, and through singing and song writing. When trauma happened to me, it was this gift of communication that was hit hard. I no longer sang. I stopped song writing. Art and creativity took a back seat. I lost the joy of creating. I couldn't sing. I didn't want to praise or worship. I couldn't find the motivation to write. Even on the days I felt a bit better, I felt like a fraud. How could I write to exhort and encourage others when I was struggling so much myself?

It took time, but I took baby steps, sometimes forwards, sometimes, frustratingly backwards. I could not sing like I did before. Instead, I sat at the piano and started practicing scales. I had always wanted to play the piano. Now I took the opportunity to start learning a little. I couldn't pick up my art like I did before. Instead, I had a desire to use my hands to make things with clay. It was then I discovered how pottery-making has become so helpful for people suffering with trauma and PTSD. I found it hard to write the long book I was writing before. Over time, I found it possible to start writing shorter books like this one, with the goal of using my experiences to help others.

Maybe you are a singer, a worshipper, a song writer, a speaker, a preacher, a teacher, an encourager and exhorter, a parent, someone who just loves to speak good things to your family and your children? Perhaps through trouble and trauma, the enemy has closed you down and shut you up? Has he shut the door between your heart and your mouth? Because of the injustice and trauma, have you lost your voice? Are you too angry and disappointed with God, yourself and others to speak the truth of His Word? Has the enemy succeeded in silencing you?

If the answer is yes, you need to do something. And it needs to be different to what you *are* doing. You need to do something different to break out of the crippling cage the enemy wants to keep you in. If you can only squeak out a song, or a small word of praise, then squeak it. If you can't get out of the house because of lack of purpose and depression, just take one step out into the garden and plant a flower. If it is too hard to pray, say just one sentence of prayer or pray a prayer from a book. If trauma has silenced your voice, play what you want to say on a drum. If trauma has stolen your creativity, get out a brush and paints and start throwing paint on that paper or canvas any way you want. If trauma and PTSD have you in daily pain, speak a word of empathy to someone else who is suffering. Instead of focussing on what you cannot do, ask God what you can do, however small, and ask for His help to do it. It is all an achievement. Take a step. Cross a line. Do something. Keep living. As you keep moving, God is able to take you somewhere and help you make progress.

6. Go to the One Who Can Deliver

At a most fundamental, pivotal and spiritual level, sometimes the sin, pains, dysfunctions and traumas of our lives, and the sin and dysfunction of our families back to several generations, can give inroads and opportunities for demonic forces to be assigned against us. This can happen through occult involvement, Satan worship, witchcraft, freemasonry, spiritualism, clairvoyancy, some tribal occult practices, addictions, and trauma. If you are experiencing repeated traumas, patterns of abuse and trauma, the feeling that every time you make positive headway you are stopped in your tracks, a continued sense of confusion, oppression, suppression, old sins and negative habits resurfacing, destructive thought patterns, suicidal thoughts, hopelessness, despair, doubt and loss of trust in God, attacks on your marriage, argumentativeness, extreme anger, violent behaviour and other destructive emotions you are finding are hard to control, it may be that there is demonic influence particularly targeting you to destroy you. Trauma can give it a greater opportunity to work destructively.

However, now you know of that possibility, you have been warned and armed with knowledge. If you know who you are in Christ and how to use your authority, do it right now. You can tell satanic influences to stop what they are doing and leave, in the name of Jesus, the one who died and rose again, and you can speak the cleansing blood of Jesus over your mind and heart. If you don't know how to do that, get with another believer who can show you how and do it with you. If you are not a believer in Jesus, only He is the one who can deliver people from demonic attack and influence. He wants to help you and set you free.

Some ministers have a lot of experience in praying with people who are influenced in this way and recognising, dealing with, rooting out, and destroying demonic activity. That does not mean it will be dramatic. It can be very gentle and honouring of you as a person. In the back of this book, among other resources, I have suggested possible ministries for this purpose. Or you can approach a church minister and ask them to pray with and for you.

7. Remember – It Is Not in Vain

Jesus suffered the most terrible trauma of betrayal, being lied about, abused, taunted, tortured, and killed. Knowing He was going to die in a horrific way, to take away our sins, He knelt and prayed in the garden, asking God to remove the cup of suffering He would have to endure. Such was His agony that He sweated drops of blood. Then came the beatings, the insults, pain, humiliation, and crucifixion. It looked so much like the forces of darkness had won. But His death was intentional. It was for the joy set before Him that He endured the Cross for our sake so that *we* would not suffer the punishment of sin.

God planned a way for men and women to be set free. Jesus did not suffer this agony and die in vain. His wounds were not in vain. The trauma He went through paid for us to be sin-free, and to be joined once again in relationship with the Father. It's not the same as it was in a sense. That relationship is no longer in a beautiful, perfect garden but in this fallen world where trauma happens. But the relationship is still the same one of a loving Father who cares for His beloved children.

Joseph's wounds were not in vain. Many years later, when his brothers arrived in Egypt during a famine to buy grain, they did not recognise him, but he recognised them. At one point, unknown to them, he was overwhelmed with emotion and tears and had to leave the room. The memories, all he endured, the years of missing his father and mother, the death of his mother while he was gone, the prison sentence, the hardship, the fear for his life, the lies and betrayal, the trauma – it all came flooding back to him in images so clear they could have happened yesterday. Yet his wounds were not in vain. His ultimate position of great influence in Egypt supplied not only Egypt and the surrounding lands with food during seven years of famine, but provided for and fed his own family and kept them alive.

Naomi's wounds – what did they do? Weren't they in vain? It may seem so. But as Boaz and Ruth walked together in the evening light and she watched over her grandson, perhaps she felt glad for the love Boaz and Ruth had found in each other, glad for the health of the growing family, and the wisdom of life she was able to pass on to Ruth and the little one.

When my mother died from cancer and I had had so little time with her in life I was devastated. I was only thirty years old. I had lived with her for only the first few years up until I was three, and from the age of fourteen to sixteen. Now she was gone. It felt like my life had been so full of trauma. I cried out to the Lord, 'I'm supposed to be helping others, but I feel so disadvantaged!' There was a pause and He said, 'Yes, you are. But I am turning your disadvantages into your advantages.' What did He mean? Those very things I had suffered would, in some way, be used to help others, who would then go on to help others. Are my wounds in vain? Not if they are helping you now.

And your wounds? Don't let them be in vain. Use them. Your scars are part of your authority. With them you have a greater credibility, a deeper empathy, a wiser word, a kinder heart, an anointing to bring healing to others who are hurting in our world. Somehow, the suffering you have experienced is not in vain. The following scripture isn't just speaking of Jesus. It is speaking of all those who believe in Him.

> 'The Spirit of the Lord God is upon me, because the
> Lord has anointed and qualified me to preach the
> Gospel of good tidings to the meek, the poor, and

afflicted; He has sent me to bind up and heal the broken hearted, to proclaim liberty to the physical and spiritual captives and the opening of the prison to those who are bound, to proclaim the acceptable year of the Lord (the year of His favour) and the day of vengeance of our God, to comfort all who mourn, to grant consolation and joy to those who mourn in Zion – to give them an ornament of beauty instead of ashes, the oil of joy instead of mourning, the garment of praise instead of a heavy, burdened, failing spirit – that they might be called oaks of righteousness, lofty, strong, and magnificent, distinguished for uprightness, justice, and right standing with God, the planting of the Lord that He may be glorified, and they shall rebuild the ancient ruins; they shall raise up the former desolations and renew the ruined cities, the devastations of former generations...You shall be called the priests of the Lord; people will speak of you as the ministers of our God.[72]

Your own grieving and mourning and your knowledge of how it feels to have a failing spirit will enable you to have so much more understanding of others, and how to minister to them. You can become like a tree, strong, an oak of righteousness, able to help rebuild the lives of others. No matter how it looks and feels, that is the truth of who you are, and who your experience will help others to be.

Now we have completed our look at the spiritual steps, let's look at the final very practical and very important chapter on those experiencing trauma and PTSD. What to do, and what not to do, if we truly want to help them.

Chapter 6

Helping Others in Trauma & with PTSD

'If you try to handle the trauma of others in ignorance of its impact and without knowing how to respond, you will damage those who are already severely hurt.'
- Diane Langberg

Suffering after-effects from trauma, and suffering from PTSD or C-PTSD does not mean the person is weak, or weaker than someone else. A person should never be made to feel they are weak because of the way trauma has affected them. They should never be made to feel that they are useless. Never say 'what is your problem?', or, 'I am okay, why aren't you?' Never think *you* would do better than them if you were in *their* situation.

We worked with a couple leading a Christian mission base in the USA for a time. A shocking event in our family affected family members leaving us deeply traumatised. Then, I injured my arm. After travelling thousands of miles across the States to get time with our children, the injury turned into a severe case of Adhesive Capsulitis, also known as frozen shoulder, an extremely painful condition that immobilises normal use in the arm and shoulder, and makes sleeping difficult. I had a very bad case. It required pain medication and anti-inflammatories twenty-four hours a day. I couldn't function normally, and could barely dress or undress or perform other daily tasks. Every movement was excruciating. To gain back use of the arm and shoulder, I had to do intensive and painful exercises three times a day. Doing these exercises was like going through self-inflicted torture. It can take up to two years to recover fully. Without the necessary exercise and help, many people do not regain full mobility of the arm.

While all this was happening, we were suffering the terrible effects of the trauma in our family. At the same time, I was experiencing menopause symptoms, having debilitating hot flushes from the changes in hormones levels day and night. I felt like everything was in pain, physically, emotionally and spiritually. I was deeply traumatised and trying to help bring a sense of equilibrium to the rest of the family when I felt like dying myself.

Fortunately, a pastor in the area put us in touch with a chiropractor and others connected us with a physiotherapist. Both were willing to give free treatment and were a great help. Our daughter, being a skilled massage therapist, made a huge difference. If it had not been for the kindness of these people, I don't know what condition I would be in today.

The leadership couple back on the other side of the country demanded unnecessarily that we return immediately. They could have changed our teaching schedule to a later date but they didn't want to wait for me to improve before travelling back over two thousand miles by car. Once there, I would not be able to get free treatment, and we did not have the money to pay for the amount of help required. One of them said insensitively in an email that they had 'once had an arm issue' which was fine after a couple of visits to the physiotherapist. We had no idea what condition they had suffered, but it was certainly not the same as the one I was suffering!

Their approach was thoughtless given the degree of trauma and pain I was experiencing. It lacked empathy and understanding. There are several negative underlying messages that could be read from their response. One of them is, 'I managed when I had a problem. Why can't you?'; 'Why don't you do what I did and then you will be fine.' The message here is that everyone should respond the same way. It takes no account of what another person is suffering and says, in other words, 'Why aren't you as strong as I am?' Insensitive people try to give quick-fix solutions that are inappropriate for the person suffering trauma.

We should never do that to people suffering trauma. We should not make them feel ashamed for where they are at, make them feel that they are not doing enough, give the impression that we would manage better if we were in their shoes, or make them feel that they are not as strong as we are. Unless you have been through debilitating trauma yourself, you cannot expect others to do what *you think* you would do if you were in the same situation, because you have no clue how you would respond unless you are actually that same person in that situation yourself!

You should not make the person feel weak because they aren't coping as well as others, or as well as you think they ought to be, or as well as you think you would.

Ignorance

I have met many people who have no clue what to say to people suffering trauma. There are people who have no idea what you are going through, yet they will take no time to understand the situation, ask no questions, and will form all sorts of opinions about what happened, what you should do, how you should feel, and say things that are very disabling and even dangerous to a suffering person. There is no excuse for this. In our world where there is so much trauma and suffering, it is important to learn what we can about how to respond well. There is so much more understanding than years ago in the area of mental health and well-being, and we have access to masses of information and learning opportunities via books, the internet, workshops and training courses. If you have been through trauma yourself, you will have learned many of these things through your experience. For those who are close to someone going through trauma, you cannot understand in the same way, but you can learn how to be sensitive and how to communicate better. For those who just want to learn because trauma is prevalent in our world, you will be better prepared to help when you are put into that position.

Here are some things that are unhelpful and should *not* be communicated to people suffering trauma.

DON'T:

- Give easy pat answers or tell the person that everything is going to be okay
- Offer unsolicited advice or tell the person what they 'should' do
- Blame the person's trauma or C/PTSD for your relationship or family problems
- Invalidate, minimize, or deny the person's experience
- Tell the person to 'get over it' or 'snap out of it'
- Quote scriptures as if that should make the person feel better. Scriptures can have what is known as the 'splat' effect where they will hit the person but not be able to penetrate because of the trauma[73]
- Make out that you would manage the situation better than them if it had happened to you

- Give ultimatums or make threats or demands to get them to change how they feel
- Tell the person they should be grateful it wasn't worse
- Take over with your own personal experiences or feelings
- Add further stress and pressure to what they are dealing with.

If you are the relative, friend, employer or acquaintance of someone who has been through trauma and/or has C/PTSD, here are some helpful tips on what to say and what not to say.

Things Not to Say[74]

- *'I know how you feel.'* Although your words may have good intentions, it is impossible for you to know exactly how they feel unless you have experienced the same situation. Even then, you still wouldn't feel exactly the same because you are a different person and everyone handles experiences differently.
- *'You're strong so you'll be fine.'* This communicates an expectation that the person will get over the trauma soon, which is unhelpful. For someone with PTSD, every day can be a battle, and it is very possible that they may not feel strong at all. It can create guilt that they are not living up to something they should.
- *'It could have been worse.' 'What happened to you was not that bad.'* Whether this is true or not, it doesn't help the person who has experienced something very terrible. It simply could not have been worse to them.

- *'If you keep dwelling on it you'll never move on.'* The nature of trauma and PTSD is that your mind dwells involuntarily on what happened. It is not something you can switch off when you choose.
- *'You are past that now so move on.'* Telling someone with PTSD to 'move on' is insensitive and unhelpful. I actually cannot stand that phrase and would never use it with a person in trauma. Many people are having to learn how to survive each hour of each day and the phrase 'move on' expects them to just forget about what happened and be able to leave it behind. Believe me, they would love to, but traumatized people cannot be expected to work to a particular timetable.
- *'Shouldn't you be better by now?'* Another insensitive remark.
- *'People have been through worse.'* Comparisons with other people are best avoided as trauma affects people differently. This phrase invalidates what they are going through.
- *'I thought only soldiers got that.'* No, PTSD can happen to anybody and develop after many different traumatic experiences.
- *'You are so negative.'*
- *'Stop being a victim because you are a survivor.'*
- *'When will you stop being depressed?'*
- *'Why didn't you tell me sooner?'*
- *'You can do better than this.'*
- *'Go and get psychiatric help because something is wrong.'* It would be better to talk with them about the possibility of help in a very positive way, and be prepared to go with them and support them.
- *'I have given up on you.'*

- *'God doesn't give you what you can't handle.'* This is not actually true. There are times when things happen in life that are definitely too much to handle. It is not helpful to involve God in the event in this way. Saying something like, 'God is with you. He knows what happened. He is deeply grieved that this happened. He understands (He does) and is hurting too; and He's with you now. Lean on Him.' would be more helpful.

Things to Say

- *'I don't know what it is like to have PTSD, but I am here for you. I'll support you.'* When someone has PTSD, they don't feel like anyone understands. It is true that most people will not understand because most have not experienced PTSD. So just telling them that you support them can bring them comfort.
- *'How can I help?'* Typically, the person suffering thinks there is nothing you can do to help, but it is good for them to hear on a regular basis that there is someone who cares and truly wants to help. And one day they may come up with something that would be a help to them. If you offer help, be prepared to keep your word.
- *'Please help me understand how you feel.'*
- *'What can I do to help you feel less stressed?'* This might include scheduling appointments, doing homework, cooking meals, running errands, looking after the children, or anything that will help relieve stress they may be feeling.
- *'If you need to talk, I'll listen.'* Give the choice and opportunity to share, if wanted. Be a good listener.

- *'Let's do something to clear your mind.'* Encouraging the person to do an activity can really help give them something positive and constructive to do, and provide a healthy and enjoyable distraction from thinking through the trauma they have experienced. Coming up with ideas and doing it together is an extra motivation when they may not have the ability to motivate themselves, or do it by themselves.

- *'What happened to you was not your fault.'* It is really important for the person to be reassured that they were not responsible for what happened. And, it was certainly not deserved! We had insensitive and ignorant people tell us that the traumatic event we experienced was probably partly caused by us because there are always 'two sides' to every story. This is not true. There are not always two sides. Both parties are not always at fault. Sometimes people do terrible things to others that are completely undeserved. Never tell a traumatised person that something was their fault. You should never make these judgements and especially when you don't know and are not prepared to find out the facts. You could add unbearable pain to someone and push them over an edge on which they are already sitting precariously.

- *'This isn't fair.'*

- *'What happened to you should never have happened and you did not deserve that.'*

- *'You are not weak or bad or wrong. You didn't deserve this and you could not have stopped it.'*

- *'It's okay to be hurt and angry. These feelings don't make you a bad person.'*

- *'I believe in you.'* It is vital that the person knows they are not a lost cause and that they have people who still support and believe in them.
- *'I love you and I wish I could take the pain away.'*
- *'I am proud of you/your courage/strength.'*
- *'I'm so sorry they hurt you.'*
- *'How can I help you feel safe?'* Trauma alters the way a person perceives the world and it can now appear to be a frightening place. It also damages a person's ability to trust. Anything that can be done to rebuild the person's sense of security and safety will contribute to their recovery. Don't do everything for them but help them to regain self-confidence and self-trust.
- *'I won't preach forgiveness at you.'* And it may be better not to say that phrase at all if you are using it as a way to subtly highlight the idea of forgiveness! While forgiveness may be helpful on the part of the sufferer, it is not something to demand from them, and needs working through in a manner appropriate for them and to a timescale they can manage for it to be genuine. Never, ever suggest to someone who has just been through trauma that they forgive (see section on forgiveness in Chapter 5 – Spiritual Steps).
- *'You are not alone, no matter how much it feels like it.'* Make sure you back that statement up with action.

When Support is Lacking

The support of family and friends is critical when someone is coming to terms with a traumatic event. Their presence and support, or lack of presence and support, can have a huge effect on the person who is suffering. If the trauma has left someone suicidal, their support can even make a difference between life and death.

However, sometimes it can be a terrible shock and an added trauma to discover that those people who could or should support you may not live up to your expectations. Just at a time when you need it the most, the results of trauma are exacerbated when you don't get the support from key people in your life. That lack of support can be expressed and felt in different ways:

- **Embarrassment, Avoidance & Silence**: Some people may give the impression that they are avoiding you. Perhaps your devastating situation embarrasses them in some way and they just don't know what to say, so they say nothing. Unfortunately, when friends say nothing, it speaks very loud negative messages that they do not really care. Avoidance and silence from others can be very cruel to the person who is traumatised.

- **Ignoring the Issue:** Some people won't communicate with you about the issue; they avoid talking about it. It becomes the 'elephant in the room', a massive issue which is never discussed but which is always there in the background.

- **Ignorant Input:** Some people endeavour to talk and be supportive but what they say is not helpful and can sometimes make things worse. This maybe because of a lack of understanding about how to talk with people in trauma; because they haven't experienced trauma themselves; because of thoughtlessness; because they haven't genuinely tried to put themselves in the victim's shoes; they haven't really thought it through; or perhaps, because of their faith they are used to quoting certain scriptures or phrases instead of learning how to relate to suffering. In any case, their 'support' is well-intentioned but can be detrimental.

- **Not knowing the Facts:** Some people don't want to know the facts or details but want to comment on the situation. This is a lack of supportive skills at the most basic level. These people have not earned the right to comment.

- **Comparison & Guilt Creating:** There can also be people who expect you to handle a situation in the way they think they would handle the situation, although they have no personal experience of what you are dealing with. Instead of giving support, they place the burden of expectation on you, and the guilt that you are not managing the traumatic situation better.

- **Sympathise with the Abuser:** Sometimes, it can be because people sympathise with and feel sorry for the perpetrator of the trauma more than they do you as the victim. Strangely this does happen. A lack of understanding about the situation, a refusal to find out what happened, subsequent ignorance, assumptions about your involvement – all of these can mean that you don't receive the support you need as the victim, while the perpetrator gets off 'scot-free', or even gains sympathy. This is wrong.

- **Victim blaming and shaming:** This occurs when instead of affirming what has been done to you is wrong, they focus on your inability to pull yourself together. They will say things like, 'Move on', 'What's your problem?', 'You should be over this by now.' 'Surely what they did to you wasn't that bad', 'You should forgive them'. They may even go so far as to say things that are actually supportive of the person whose action caused the trauma.

Just at a time when the wrong done to you needs to be acknowledged, you are blamed instead for your part in contributing to the event that caused the trauma, even if you did nothing, or little, wrong. It is assumed that a negative event always has 'two sides' even if you contributed nothing to cause it. Perhaps you are told that the rape you experienced was because you were wearing a tight t-shirt or walking alone. Perhaps relatives refuse to believe that a loved one could be responsible for the trauma they have caused others in the family, or because you are an adult and the perpetrator is a child and they naturally feel sorry for the child and blame the adult, even if that is incorrect. Parents are often blamed and shamed simply because they are parents, even if they are not to blame. Children are sometimes blamed simply because they cannot defend themselves. Those suffering trauma are sometimes blamed and shamed based on their religion, gender or colour.

Victim shaming and blaming can be subtle or downright obvious. Whatever it looks like, it is wrong and cruel, and brings extra suffering and can be very tormenting to the traumatised person.

You are vulnerable to greater grief due to lack of support in all of these ways whether it is through absence, silence, being ignored, ignorance, assumptions, thoughtlessness, insensitivity, expectations, or blaming and shaming. There will be feelings of anger, disappointment, and disillusionment when you discover the people you thought would be supportive are not. It's the last thing you need when you are already dealing with trauma, but it does happen.

So what do you do when you find yourself in a position of non-support or insufficient or inappropriate support?

I found when talking with trained counsellors and even my local doctor, that there was greater understanding with them than there was in talking to some friends. There are also charities and/or organisations that can help, including those that specialise in dealing with specific traumas, for example, family issues, being estranged, divorce, death of a loved one, etc. There are also support groups online for specific traumas.

Try to focus on and put in place people around you who will bring good support into your life, who can understand (or at least try to understand) what you are going through, who validate you, who will not victim shame, who have personal experience of trauma, some training in trauma, or who just genuinely love and care for you and are prepared to learn. Don't be afraid to communicate and educate so that people can learn what is helpful and not helpful in how to support a traumatised person.

Providing Practical Support

After a traumatic experience, it is important to re-establish a normal routine as this will help restore a sense of predictability and control. While the person will need time and space to deal with a highly stressful event, they will also need encouragement to engage in enjoyable and constructive activities. Provide practical support to enable them to have time to rest and recover, but don't avoid inviting them to events or to contribute in some way using their gifts and talents. Even if they turn down the invitation, it is important for the person to feel needed and useful, and not be left isolated or cut-off from others, thinking they no longer have any value or purpose.

Acknowledge any achievements made, no matter how small they may appear. Encourage them to look after themselves with nutritious food, regular exercise, and plenty of rest and sleep. Help them use the tools in this book. Do things for them if necessary to give them time to get back on their feet and doing things for themselves. While they may want to isolate and spend a lot of time by themselves, it is essential that they get out. If they are unable to motivate themselves to do this, take them out shopping, see if you can get them along to an exercise group with you, do art classes with them, or some other constructive activity that will help them to meet others and take their mind off the event.

During the trauma in my own life, I lost a lot of motivation and energy. I was thankful that my husband took on the cooking and shopping. If he had left it to me, we might have starved! It took me two years to begin to engage again in some activities. Be sure to encourage people as they manage to take up activities again in their own time.

Providing Emotional Support

Never try and force people to talk about the traumatic event before they are ready. When they do want to talk, here are some suggestions which might be helpful:

- Choose a time to talk when you won't be interrupted, or feel rushed or tired.
- Reassure them that any feelings of distress are to be expected after what they experienced.

- Make another time to talk if it seems like the person is too distressed to continue.
- Don't feel that you have to make their distress go away as getting upset is a natural part of coping with a traumatic experience.
- If they want to talk but are tired of the crying induced by talking about the event, be patient and allow them to gather themselves together. While being able to cry after a traumatic event is healthy, I found that constant crying over a very long period of time added to feelings of being emotionally distraught, and made me feel like my life was miserable all the time. That didn't help. Sometimes, I wanted to talk but didn't want all the emotions wrapped up with it. If I cried, the listener would say, 'It's okay to cry.' I would say, 'No, it is not. I don't want to cry again.'
  Allow the traumatised person to decide how they want to communicate, and the level of emotion they want to express, and help them with that. They might need to cry if the trauma has numbed them. But there is no point in encouraging crying in someone who has had enough of it! Traumatised people need to be able to experience times of being able to communicate without extreme emotions, and they need to be able to experience positive, happy feelings, not just negative ones.
- Remember to actively listen, don't interrupt, and don't talk about yourself or your own experiences. Try to put yourself in their shoes.
- Show that you understand what they are saying by feeding back and re-phrasing the information they give you (e.g. 'It sounds like...' 'Did I understand correctly that...').

- Acknowledge their distress with statements such as *'It must be really hard to go through something like this'*, *"This is such a tough time for you"*, *'It's perfectly normal for you to feel like you do'*, or *'It is understandably difficult for you to imagine life getting better again'*.
- Avoid offering simple reassurances such as, *'I know how you feel'*, or *'You'll be OK.'*[75]

At the right time, teach them about the importance of self-care, and as necessary, offer the practical help and assistance needed to set them on the path to self-care (see Chapter 4).

Looking after Yourself

Supporting someone who has been through a traumatic event can take a toll on you so that your own physical, emotional and spiritual health may be affected. It is vital that you look after your own health in all these areas. Take time for yourself, engaging with other people and doing other activities that are life-giving for you. If necessary, join a support group or seek the help of a counsellor or other helpful person to give you the support you need.

When you take an aeroplane flight, the steward or stewardess gives the emergency and safety instructions before take-off. They always remind you that in the event of an emergency the pilot will release the oxygen masks and they tell you to put yours on before your child's. That is not because the child is less important, but because you cannot help the child put theirs on if you are starved of oxygen yourself. The traumatised adult is not a child because they have been through trauma. But they do need help and support. You can only give what is needed if you care for yourself first.

The traumatised deserve and need love and care. By reading this book, you will have learned important tools and skills to help them, and to help them help themselves. Your love and efforts are invaluable and precious. By recognising your own boundaries and caring for yourself, you will be a better help to them. So remember to look after yourself too.

A Final Word for those
Who have Experienced Trauma

Does the journey end? That can depend on a lot of factors including whether or not the trauma is still ongoing. At the time of completing this book, the trauma was still going on after four years, so can the journey of healing end? Learning to survive has been critical. Daily survival is the key to the journey towards a better place. It's a journey towards healing. Healing? It feels like a big word. But I have chosen to believe that it is possible. And I have chosen to take all I can from my experience to help others. Perhaps it just becomes a different journey to the one we expected. With every step we take to survive, help ourselves heal and get the help we need, we can move forward, bit by bit, to a better place in ourselves and in our lives. It may be different. But it can still be good, and maybe it can be better than we ever expected.

Whatever you have experienced and been through, and whatever challenges you face because of it, you are of inestimable value. Your life is worth it. *You* are worth it. You have so much to give. Stay on the journey. You can regain yourself and your life. Your survival, as you take the necessary steps to care for yourself, will take you day-by-day to that better place. Life IS possible again.

Stay With Me

Stay with me
on this journey.
Not the one we planned,
but one we've had to walk.
We can do it better
if we do it together,
and remember,
we are not alone.
You and I are precious people
who've known the fill of pain,
and though we may not see it yet,
good *can* come again.
We've been face to face with
darkness and trouble,
but the time has come
to believe once more that
LIFE *is* possible!

A Final Image for those Who have Experienced Trauma

I am going to share a very special image with you that helped me a great deal. You will develop your own positive images, of course, but I hope this can aid your journey.

I found myself in a boat in the stormy silence of a vast sea.
There was no land in sight and no way to get out
of the boat.
I asked myself, what do I do?
I did the only thing I could do.
Instead of gazing out onto the vastness of the sea,
I turned my eyes to what was in the boat.
What resources did I have in the boat?
What could I use?
What was immediately available?
I decided, if I have to be in this boat,
I better learn to sail it!

Acknowledgements

Many thanks go to Dr Karen Drake, Dr H Norman Wright, Kay Wells, Marsha Farmer, Michelle Duke, Linda Harding, Tina Hoffmann, Jenny Burns, Sue Allen, Galina Smith, Cathy Byers, Debbie Richens, Anja Kraijo, Rebecca Ramirez de Arellano, and all those patient people who put in effort to read, correct, review, comment on and/or endorse this book. Your insights, observations, experiences, and encouragement have been invaluable.

Thank you to the great Grace Vaughan for your tireless patience in working on book covers and minute adjustments to colour and text positioning that we kept sending your way over such a long period of time, and for doing it with joy...and grace.

Thank you to the Hopi and Navajo for allowing us on your land, especially Daniel, Genevieve and Joel, Frank and Anna for your hard work in helping us survive. It didn't work out how we thought, but we so appreciate our time with you and the opportunity to experience just a small part of your world. This book would not be the same without our time there. T'aa iiyisii ahehee.

A big thank you to those who have 'been through the fire' and appreciated the value, importance and timing of this book, and those who have known me enough and long enough to believe in the integrity and sincerity of this work.

Finally, thank you to my husband, Stuart, for your support, encouragement and experience, for reading out loud every day, editing, rearranging, uploading, waiting for my slow responses, and nudging me repeatedly to get this done! You have brought inspiration, enjoyment and purpose, and I really could not have completed this without you.

About the Author

Michelle Simpson D.Min, has experienced childhood and adult trauma, giving her profound insights into the trauma experience which are captured in this book.

With a doctorate in cross-cultural missions and natural health and nutrition (Phoenix University of Theology), she is an expert in cross-cultural living, a passionate advocate for natural health and wellbeing, and a trainer in trauma awareness. A creative communicator, she is a writer, speaker, artist and singer/songwriter.

Originally from the UK, her Christian faith has led her to share hope, love, freedom and practical help while living and serving in several nations including China, Thailand and Native America. She is ordained through Church for the Nations, Phoenix and is the co-founder of Catalyst Ministries.

Trained in Animal Assisted Therapy, Michelle loves to talk about and train dogs and take them on therapy visits to bring happiness to others. Some of her favourite things are being with family, hiking with her husband, Stuart, and their dogs, being outside enjoying nature, growing things, and sustainable living. Michelle can be contacted at:

michellesimpsonlife@gmail.com

www.loadsoflife.com

Further Resources

The inclusion of the following resources does not necessarily represent the endorsement by the author. They are offered as a few sources of information and potential support to readers on trauma and related subject matter.

Healing from Complex Trauma & PTSD/CPTSD is a website and blog by award winning and published author, Lilly Hope Lucario. It is recommended, endorsed and shared by many mental health professionals, clinicians and psychologists.
healingfromcomplextraumaandptsd.wordpress.com/

Mind, the mental health charity in the UK is another excellent site and invaluable source of information. Mind provides advice and support to empower anyone experiencing a mental health issue, including PTSD.
mind.org.uk/

The Grief Recovery Method®. This is an evidence based program to deal with the pain of emotional loss, with practical, applicable actions to feel better rather than feeling paralysed and stuck forever.
griefrecoverymethod.com/

The Body Keeps the Score: *Mind, Brain and Body in the Transformation of Trauma,* by Dr Bessel van der Kolk. This best-selling book by one of the world's foremost experts on trauma, shows how trauma literally reshapes both body and brain, compromising sufferers' capacities for pleasure, engagement, self-control, and trust. It also explores innovative treatments that offer new paths to recovery by activating the brain's natural neuroplasticity.

Beat My Addictions with Chris Hill is a 7-day plan based on an understanding of the subconscious mind and how the mind and body are affected once an addictive substance or activity is introduced. *beatmyaddictions.com/*

Escape the Maze of Spiritual Abuse: Creating *Healthy Christian Cultures,* by Dr Lisa Oakley & Justin Humphreys, Society for Promoting Christian Knowledge (SPCK), 2019

Drawing on research, testimonies and years of experience, the authors describe clearly the nature of spiritual abuse and the best ways to respond. Recovery *is* possible.

The Subtle Power of Spiritual Abuse: Recognizing *and Escaping Spiritual Manipulation and False Spiritual Authority Within the Church,* by David Johnson & Jeff VanVonderen, Bethany House Publishers, 1991

On the subject of spiritual abuse, this book is an excellent resource that highlights how spiritual abuse can take place, and how to experience true freedom.

Endnotes

---

[1] https://drgabormate.com/topic/mindbody-health/
[2] Dr Diane Langberg is a world recognised psychologist for her work specialising in the area of counselling trauma victims.
[3] H. Norman Wright, *Experiencing Grief*, published by B&H Publishing Group, 2004, chapter 1
[4] *Experiencing Grief,* 14
[5] Diane Langberg, *Suffering and the Heart of God*,
[6] https://www.nimh.nih.gov/health/topics/post-traumatic-stress-disorder-ptsd/index.shtml
[7] Section detailing PTSD symptoms taken from https://www.nimh.nih.gov/health/publications/post-traumatic-stress-disorder-ptsd/index.shtml
[8] https://www.psychologicalscience.org/news/releases/why-some-soldiers-develop-ptsd-while-others-dont.html
[9] https://www.psychologytoday.com/gb/blog/compassion-matters/201207/recognizing-complex-trauma
[10] https://www.psychologytoday.com/gb/blog/compassion-matters/201207/recognizing-complex-trauma
[11] https://developingchild.harvard.edu/science/key-concepts/
[12] See https://medicalxpress.com/news/2019-04-brain-scans-ptsd.html and https://www.ncbi.nlm.nih.gov/pmc/articles/PMC2729089/
[13] https://healingfromcomplextraumaandptsd.wordpress.com/ptsd-stress/
[14] https://www.apa.org/advocacy/interpersonal-violence/women-trauma
[15] https://www.psychologicalscience.org/news/releases/why-some-soldiers-develop-ptsd-while-others-dont.html
[16] https://www.verywellmind.com/what-is-brain-plasticity-2794886
[17] Genesis 42:36
[18] https://www.mayoclinic.org/tests-procedures/cognitive-behavioral-therapy/about/pac-20384610
[19] https://www.webmd.com/mental-health/emdr-what-is-it#1
[20] www.benenden.co.uk
[21] There are also Serotonin-Norepinephrine Reuptake inhibitors (SNRIs), Tricyclic Antidepressants (TCAs) and Monoamine Oxidase inhibitors (MAOIs).

[22] Antidepressants increase the risk of suicide, violence, and homicide at all ages (https://www.bmj.com/content/358/bmj.j3697/rr-4)
[23] For example, https://www.fooddive.com/news/study-links-junk-food-to-cancer/532988/
[24] https://www.theguardian.com/commentisfree/2012/sep/10/alzheimers-junk-food-catastrophic-effect
[25] https://www.goodhousekeeping.com/health/wellness/a25904/taste-buds-change/
[26] https://www.sleep.org/articles/ways-technology-affects-sleep/
[27] While some view this to be a myth due to a lack of clinical studies demonstrating a proven link between milk and sleep patterns, there are also many other sources that highlight the benefits of warm milk due to its tryptophan protein.
[28] Psalm 63:5-8
[29] Adapted from Psalm 127:2
[30] Psalm 94:19, AMPC
[31] David Adam, *The Edge of Glory – Prayers in the Celtic Tradition*, SPCK Publishing, 2011
[32] Arts Therapy for Self-Healing (Part One) online course, Udemy
[33] https://twitter.com/potteryptsd24
[34] https://www.depressionalliance.org/music-therapy/
[35] https://www.medicalnewstoday.com/articles/320019#how-do-binaural-beats-work
[36] Professor Joe Sempik, research fellow from Nottingham University, School of Sociology and Social Policy, who has worked with Thrive (The Society for Horticultural Therapy), the leading charity in the UK using gardening to change the lives of disabled people.
[37] Dr William Bird MBE who leads Intelligent Health (source - https://stephwalters.wordpress.com/2016/02/01/too-hip-to-love-horticulture-you-might-want-to-think-again/)
[38] Dr William Bird (GP), Principles of Social & Therapeutic Horticulture course, Thrive
[39] https://www.verywellmind.com/color-psychology-2795824
[40] For example, Thrive and other opportunities in UK and USA
[41] https://www.mentalfloss.com/article/70548/11-scientific-benefits-being-outdoors
[42] 2 Timothy 1:7
[43] 1 Corinthians 2:16
[44] Isaiah 54:17, AMPC

[45] Ephesians 6:10
[46] Psalm 46:1
[47] Mindfulness meditation originates from Buddhist teachings and pays attention to thoughts without judging or engaging with them. Mantra meditation is linked to Hindu and Buddhist traditions and involves using repetitive sounds in the hope it clears the participants' minds.
[48] For example, see https://www.bbc.co.uk/programmes/articles /2nB1psRz3JFQpzDh6J2Z6xl/is-mindfulness-meditation-dangerous
[49] https://www.sleepfoundation.org/dreams/lucid-dreams
[50] www.health.harvard.edu/mens-health/marriage-and-mens-health; https://www.psychologytoday.com/us/blog/stronger-the-broken-places/201509/6-reasons-why-married-people-should-have-better-sex-lives
[51] A good example is Lilly Hope Lucario's website - https://www.healingfromcomplextraumaandptsd.com
[52] Pantheism comes from two Greek words meaning 'all (*pan*) is God (*theos*)' and is the belief that God consists of everyone and everything. For example, a tree is God, a mountain is God, the universe is God, all people are God. God and the universe are therefore considered to be identical. Pantheism is found in many "nature" religions and New Age religions, Hinduism and Buddhism. It is also the worldview of Unity, Christian Science, and Scientology.
[53] In the New Thought philosophy, the Law of Attraction is the belief that positive or negative thoughts bring positive or negative experiences into a person's life. The belief is based on the idea that people and their thoughts are both made from pure energy, and that through the process of like energy attracting like energy a person can improve their own health, wealth, and personal relationships.
[54] Over thirty years ago, I came to believe in Jesus. It is known as being a *Christian*. I didn't adopt a religion. I came to know a person and what He has done for me. Coming to know the crucified and risen Christ, and God as my Father, made a huge difference to all the early trauma I had suffered as a child. I discovered that God was not just a belief, but the One who created me. I realised that He really cared for me and cared about all I had been through. His compassion towards me (and everyone) was huge. When I gave my life to Him, I was forgiven of sin, and filled with His love, and I found a new heart and a

new life. That relationship filled the void in my life and gave meaning and purpose to all I have been through.

[55] John 10:10

[56] 1 John 1:5

[57] Acts 10:38

[58] Mark 5:21-43

[59] Mark 9:23-24

[60] Matthew 9:20–22, Mark 5:25–34, Luke 8:43–48

[61] Psalm 27:9-14

[62] Isaiah 53:3-4, Psalm 147:3

[63] John 14:13-14

[64] Luke 10:19

[65] Based on 1 Corinthians 2:16, AMPC

[66] Philippians 4:8

[67] Psalm 8:2

[68] Psalm 8:2

[69] Matthew 18:15-17

[70] Dr Lisa Oakley & Justin Humphreys, *Escaping the Maze of Spiritual Abuse: Creating Healthy Spiritual Cultures*, SPCK Publishing, 2019, 99

[71] Psalm 18: 4-6, 28-35 , AMPC

[72] Isaiah 61:1-4, 6, AMPC

[73] Diane Langberg, https://www.tenth.org/resource-library/lectures/questions-answers-and-conclusions

[74] Some of this section is drawn from https://www.healthfaithstrength.com/10-things-to-say-to-someone-with-ptsd-and-10-things-not-to-say/

[75] http://phoenixaustralia.org/recovery/helping-others/